First Question: "You're a *what?* A vegan? What's that?"
Second Question: "Oh." Pause. "Well then, *what do you eat?*"

What do we vegans eat, anyway? Well, we're generally not out in the back yard nibbling on shrubs and grass, as some people I talk to half-seriously suggest. However, we also don't eat the same things most people sit down to dinner to, either, so explanations are needed. This cookbook in part serves as an explanation for us, but it is also designed for other purposes.

For one, it is written for vegetarians and especially sickly vegans who aren't exactly satisfied with their diet. Eating rice and ramen for days on end gets old real quick, and unfortunately lots of malnourished vegans are subsisting on such a diet' as I write this. If you already have the lofty moral principles and feel it's high time your diet (and health!) matched up to them, hopefully this cookbook will help. Giving up veganism cos you "couldn't find anything good to eat" is no excuse!

Secondly, we want to interest people in veganism and hopefully encourage them to make the switch. We won't bullshit you; this cookbook is blatant propaganda. Our message is simple: GO VEGAN! It's not a unique message: anyone faintly in touch with punk rock or animal rights has certainly heard it before. Many people have seen the gory photos, read the reasoned arguments, read the impassioned pleas, and read the facts on how veganism saves the environment and animals and one's health. Perhaps many of these people are sympathetic or they even agree that veganism is a sounder, more compassionate ethical choice than vegetarianism or being carnivorous. But they're still not vegan. This cookbook is especially designed for you foks. You've already read the cold hard facts and you've been scolded for your callousness and ignorance; we're trying a different approach. With *Soy Not Oi!* we want to go beyond the largely negative arguments for veganism and show you concretely and positively that not only is veganism politically correct, it's a lot of goddamn fun! So, instead of telling you horrible tales of cows, calves, rape racks, poisons, and profits, we're going to tell you how to make some tasty vegan food.

Finally, veganism--for me at least--is a great way to say Fuck You! to the powers that be and their advertisers, as well as being an important element to an alternative, even oppositional lifestyle. Our 9-5 rush-rush lives have squeezed out the joy of cooking and turned it into a chore, leading people to prefer microwaving a box of mash potato flakes instead of preparing a full, well-rounded meal (for about the same cost!). By separating life into work and leisure, we find ourselves with no time to even feed ourselves properly. With this cookbook, we hope to not only help you make delicious vegan food but to reclaim the art and joy of cooking that has been stripped away from us over the years by our anomic/anemic, postindustrial hyperstress culture. Instead of lives of work/leisure, we want to *play*, all the time, all our lives, and cooking can be a wonderful way to play. By cooking a good meal (especially among friends and family) and enjoying the process of cooking as much as the final product, we not only feed ourselves well, we reclaim a part of our lives that is quickly dwindling, replaced by TV, 60-hour work weeks, and "life in the fast lane." Save the earth, save animals, help yourself, and give those capitalist bastards a good kick in the Liberal Humanist ass at the same time: Cook vegan!

P.S. No apologies for the title and cover. Oi! sucks and so do the Nazis who listen to it. Granted, not all Oi! fans are boneheads, but those who aren't idiots won't be upset with the title, anyway. It's all part of the "H" word. Y'know, Humor?

P.P.S. Sorry for all the spelling and grammatical errors, but we cursorily proofread a lot of this so we could get the damn thing finished!

Your Servers:
jack&joel: editorial and general shitwork
Eryc S!@#$%&*!: all art and main recipe taster

Chef's List:
Special thanks go out to all people who graciously donated recipes (especially Jackie Weltman, Todd/Pollution Circus, Donna, and Christy), those who contributed articles (Dan/Profane Existence, Timojhen, Tom Scut, Jason,and Missy Bushwhacker, Tammy/TTU), Fred for the printing, the Hippycore/Hopeful Monsters gang for the collating, and of course Eryc for all the fantastic artwork he did. For a guy with no hair and a bottomless stomach, Eryc ain't so bad.

Table of Contents

NO-NO's

When first going vegan, shopping can be a bit tough. You have to read all the labels to see what's cool and what's not and you have to undergo the temporary pain of giving up some of your once-favorite foods. ("What? No more Cheetos?" "Whaddya mean Little Debbie Cakes have whey in them?" "Isn't at least *one* brand of chocolate chip cookie vegan?")

Further, when dutifully checking those labels, you might not even know what some of the ingredients are. Of course, it's always a good idea to avoid products with book-length ingredient lists or that contain ingredients whose names you can't pronounce, but what about stuff like casein or cocoa butter? (The latter is vegan, the former not.) Through trial and error and talks with other vegan friends, Jack and I have come up with a short list of nonvegan no-no's to watch for when shopping. This is by no means comprehensive, but it does include most of the more common nonvegan naughties.

Gelatin: Used in jello, marshmallows, candies like Starburst, Skittles, Gummy Bears, etc. This stuff is made of animal tissue (I've heard it comes from the bone marrow of horses sometimes!), so it's not even vegetarian. Also used for developing film.

Whey: Used in cookies, candy bars, chips, crackers, breads and a myriad of other baking goods, this little bastard of an ingredient seems to slip into every tasty sweet thing that would otherwise be vegan. A most frustrating ingredient because it occurs so frequently in this way, whey is the part left when cow's milk is coagulated (like to make cheese or butter).

Casein: This is a product made when milk is heated with an acid, like lactic acid. This stuff mostly occurs in "no-lactose" soy cheeses like Soyco or Soy Kaas. The labels say "lactose-free" (lactose is another milk derivative), but that doesn't mean they are therefore vegan, as we used to incorrectly assume. Soymage soy cheese is 100% vegan, but it's kind of gross. Casein is also used in plastics, adhesives, and paint manufacturing.

Caseinate: Casein mixed with a metal, like calcium caseinate or sodium caseinate.

Stearate: This usually comes in the form of *calcium stearate*, and it is found in hard candies like Gobstoppers and Sweetarts as well as other places. It comes from stearic acid, which usually is derived from tallow, or animal fat. Stearate is also used in vinyls (like car seats) and plastics.

Calcium phosphate: This is often used in English muffins, breads, cereals, and other baked goods as a preservative. Preservatives are shitty enough, but this one is really just a fancy word for ground up animal bones and teeth.

Rennet: This stuff is mostly used to curdle milk to make cheese, so it's not an ingredient vegans often trip over, but it does slip into stuff here and there. Basically, rennet is the lining of the stomach of an unweaned calf. Absolutely fucking gross, huh. Tell that to your veggie friends next time they're feasting on a pizza, as virtually all cheese is curdled with rennet, meaning that in reality cheese isn't even vegetarian.

Margarine: Of course most everyone knows what this is, but is it vegan or not? Most brands of margarine aren't vegan, but Fleischmann's in a green box is. Check around for other possible brands; you can also get soy margarine at any health food store/co-op.

There are other things that pose problems as well. For example, *maple syrup, sugar* (white, brown, powdered), and *vinegar* all use animal parts in their processing. For maple syrup, it's often a few drops of pork fat when the sap is being processed into syrup. For sugar, I believe it's ground and burnt animal bones used in refining the cane. We have included recipes in this cookbook that contain these ingredients partly because we ourselves learned of these revelations only recently, when the cookbook was well underway (thanks Jason and Todd!); partly because most of the folks who submitted recipes also didn't know this and we didn't want to turn away so many good recipes from sincere people because of this; and perhaps most importantly because unlike going vegetarian, going vegan has no ceiling, no upper limit. It is impossible to be 100% vegan and cruelty-free. Going vegan and continually building on your vegan lifestyle is a growing process, and by eliminating such "staples" as sugar and vinegar, we felt that we risked turning some people off by setting the standards too high. After all, giving up dairy is tough enough (it's actually not very difficult at all, as you'll hopefully soon see), but giving up sugar, too? Jack and I both just learned of this knowledge ourselves, and we've been vegans for several years, so it would seem a bit hypocritical for us to demand others to give up sugar immediately, although we wholeheartedly applaud anyone who does. (Incidentally, some cruelty-free sugars are unrefined sugar, like Turbanado, or something like Sucanat, though I probably spelled those words wrong.) Like we said, veganism is a lifelong growing experience. Minimally, it means refusing to eat meat, dairy and other animal byproducts, as well as refusing to wear them. This cookbook starts at that minimal level. How far you wish to take your vegan lifestyle is up to you. All we can do is offer encouragement and applaud your efforts.

VEGAN SOURCES OF NUTRIENTS

ZINC
nuts
seeds
wheat germ
brewers yeast
whole grains
yellow and green veggies
yellow fruits

MANGANESE
alfalfa
chlorophyl
wheat germ
whole grains

IODINE
dried beans
asparagus
green veggies
pineapple

COPPER
nuts
dried peas
beans
wheat bran
whole wheat
molasses
moshrooms
avocadoes
broccoli

CALCIUM
watercress
rhubarb
beets
parsley
spinach
broccoli
chinese cabbage
raw onions
raw celery
okra
chives
raw cabbage
cucumbers
turnips
zucchini
green beans
squash
artichokes

VITAMIN C
Bell Peppers
Guavas
Peppers
broccoli
watercress
parsley
radishes
asparagus
brussel sprouts
chives
strawberries
papayas
cantelopes
oranges
grapefruit

B12
Brewers Yeast
bakers yeast
rice bran
wheat germ
sunflower seeds
cornflakes
pinon nuts
soy milk
sesame seeds
Brazil nuts
Peanuts

VITAMIN D
mild exposure to
sunlight
sunflower seeds
moshrooms

PROTEIN
soya grits
gluten flour
bakers yeast
brewers yeast
soy (not oi) flour
soy beans
soy milk
pine nuts
peanuts
wheat germ
lentils

VITAMIN E
wheat and rice germ
whole wheat grains
leafy greens
nuts
seeds
legumes

VITAMIN A
peppers
parsley
carrots
sweet potatoes
apricots
spinach
mangoes
chives
squash

(INFO TAKEN FROM MINIMAX by Dr. David A. Phillips)

Obvious Stuff

Not to insult your intelligence, but here are a few things that are vegan and make for good, quick eating:

Beans, bean burros (Rosarita's Vegetarian Refrieds, or make your own), rice, peanut butter and jelly sandwiches, bagels, fruit, vegetables, certain kinds of ramen (usually oriental flavor), tomato soup (don't buy Campbell's--they slash and burn rainforests), vegetarian vegetable soup, Nature's Burger burgers, Rice Dream (as good as ice cream), Soymage sour "cream", lots of types of crackers, chips and salsa, matzos (thanks Jack), nuts, cereal and soymilk, popcorn, cous cous (kinda like rice), oatmeal, tabouli, cream of wheat, dark chocolate, pasta and spaghetti sauce (read the labels!), vegetarian beans, S&W Chili Beans (really good), Tofu Pups (tastes so much like hot dogs it's almost too scary), sourdough bread, most good breads, pita bread, cheap chocolate syrup and soymilk, fruit juice, and of course Red Vines licorice.

ESSENTIALS

Christy Colcord sez:

I definitely recommend <u>The Vegan Health Plan</u> by Amanda Sweet. It's available from the Vegan Society (UK) at 33-35 George Street, Oxford, OX1 2AY, England. It's only 5 pounds (plus some amount of postage for overseas) and it is basically the bible of all sensible vegans in the UK. The first half of the book is how to go vegan, why, and absolutely intricate descriptions, directions and possible uses for every type of bean, vegetable, spice, and vegan substitute in the natural world. The second half is recipes--really good basic recipes for everyday eating, not ones you'll use once on the folks. It is really vital to doing it right.

Write Christy at First Floor Flat, 4 Oakland Road, Redland, Bristol, BS6 6ND, England. She books low budget punkasfuck tours for North American bands, so bands with the DIY spirit interested in touring Europe and/or the UK for fun and not profit should write.

Soy Milk Like Mom Used to Make (If You Were Lucky) by Christy

<u>Soak:</u> Rinse 2 1/2 cups soybeans and soak overnight in five cups of cold water for 8-10 hours.

<u>Grind:</u> Combine in a blender one cup soaked soybeans and 2 1/2 cups of warm water. Blend for about one minute. Pour contents into a heavy pot. Repeat until all beans are blended.

<u>Cook:</u> Bring to a boil over medium heat. Turn down immediately and simmer for 20 minutes.

<u>Strain:</u> Strain the soy milk through a cloth-lined colander (you can use cheesecloth or anything with small holes). Squeeze as much liquid as possible out of the pulp by twisting the cloth tightly closed and pressing on it with a spoon. Open the cloth and stir in two cups of boiling water to rinse through any remaining milk. You can use the pulp in cooking other things, like roasts, etc. It's total protein. Some of my friends think it tastes like turkey white meat and use it on sandwiches with mustard and soyannaise.

<u>Cool:</u> The quicker the milk is cooled and the cooler it's kept, the longer it will last. Put the milk directly into bottles or jars and stand in a sink of cold water until cool, then refrigerate. It should last 5 days refrigerated.

This will make more milk than you could ever use, so I would suggest making some:

Tofu   by Christy, of course

Follow the soy milk directions, but use three cups of water for every cup of pre-soaked soy beans (when you're blending). (This isn't absolutely necessary if you've already got the milk made.) After straining the soy milk and keeping it hot, prepare the solidifier. You can use 1 1/2-2 teaspoons epsom salts or 1/4 cup vinegar or 1/4 cup lemon juice, but I prefer the lemon juice.

Start stirring the still hot soy milk in a circular motion and add half the solidifier.

Sprinkle a small amount of the remaining solidifier over the top of the milk and quickly cover with a well-fitting lid. Let the soy milk stand undisturbed for five minutes.

It's going to start to curdle into lumps of white tofu. The end result should be curds of tofu floating in a clear yellow liquid called "whey." After five minutes, if the soy milk (future whey) is still looking milky, poke at the top layer and add the rest of the solidifier gently, to avoid breaking up the curds. cover with the lid and leave to stand for a few more minutes. It might still need more solidifier, so don't worry, just put some more in and let it sit until it's all either curd or whey.

Okay, now the tofu is ready to be pressed. If you don't have a press, you can make one with any cylindrical plastic container. Poke

lots of holes in it, then line the press with a piece of muslin (cheesecloth, whatever) and pour the whey and curds in it.

Place a tight-fitting plate inside the container and get something relatively heavy on it. Let it sit for 30 minutes. Make sure to put it in the sink. When it's drained, put the tofu into a container and cover with cold water. Change water daily and it'll keep for a week. You can freeze it, too!

STEVE AND HARMONIES WHEAT GLUTON (WHEAT MEAT MATE)

Let me say that Steve Slime and Harmonie prepared this for us at a nice dinner party we had a while back and it was incredible. Nuff said.

3 pounds whole wheat flour
water
about 1 cup peanut butter (melted)
about 3 tablespoons paprika
1 onion (chopped and sauteed)
3 cups barbecue sauce

Mix flour in bowl with enough water to make it doughy (like bread dough). Form it into a ball and soak it in water for about one hour. (make sure dough is completely covered). Rinse starch and wheat flakes out of dough under faucet. Dough will shrink to about 1/3 original size and consistency should be rubbery. Add paprika, onion, and P-butter and mix. Pour in BBQ sauce, mix again. Form into patties and put on greased cookie sheet. Pour more BBQ sauce on top. Bake at 400F about 25 minutes.

Bread   by joel, who ripped it off from *Vegetarian   Times   Cookbook*
        Tunes: The Clash "London Calling"
                Dissent "Epitome of Democracy"

1   tablespoon yeast
1/2 cup lukewarm water
1 teaspoon honey (optional)
3/4   cup lukewarm water
1 tablespoon honey
3 cups unbleached white flour
1 tablespoon margarine

This recipe is fun on a warm afternoon when you're in the mood to bake. Put on that classic Clash 2LP and sprinkle the packet of yeast on the 1/2 cup of water and teaspoon of honey. Let it sit for about ten minutes; this allows you to see if the yeast is active (it shoud foam up).

Mix the 3/4 cup water, flour, honey, and oil in a big bowl, then add the yeast and mix well.

Clean your counter. Lightly sprinkle flour on it and plop the dough down on it. Knead well for about 5-7 minutes. Put dough in a lightly oiled bowl to prevent the dough from sticking. Cover with a clean towel and let rise until the dough is about doubled in size (around 35-45 minutes).

After it has risen once, punch it down and let rise again to twice its original size (about 30 minutes).

After it has risen a second time, grease a couple bread pans (2 or 3, depending on how big you want your loaves to be). If you don't have bread pans, grease a cookie sheet. Divide the dough in equal portions and put in the pans/on the sheet (the dough should fill about half of the bread pan). Let rise, uncovered, for an hour and a half. Bake at 400 degrees until golden brown, about 20-25 minutes.

Note: This recipe makes 2-3 loaves max, which isn't much, so I always either double the proportions or make at least two batches, sometimes more.

Roux   by joel
Tunes: Subvert 7"

margarine
flour

I've already   given directions in other recipes on how to make roux and what it's for, but I thought I'd repeat it in separate form.

Basically, roux is a superb thickening agent. It can be used to thicken sauces, soups, gravies, and whatever else you might want. The stuff keeps for weeks without going bad, so you can make a lot at one time and use as needed, plus it's remarkably easy to make.

First, put whatever amount of margarine you want into a saucepan and melt. Add an equal amount of flour and stir quickly. The resulting mixture should be almost like playdough in consistency and amber in color; if not add more flour. Keep cooking even when it's reached the proper consistency; the longer it cooks the more effective a thickener it will be. Cook for a few minutes and then it's done.

To thicken something, add roux to the pot of whatever slowly, spoonful by spoonful, until it reaches the desired consistency.

Store the unused roux in a covered container. Refrigerating would probably be a good idea, but not imperative.

Unbelievable Amazing Southwestern-Style Spice Mix
by Jackie Weltman

For flavoring, grilling (especially), and heartier dishes.
Warning: becomes addictive!

Combine in a food processor or a mortar and pestle and grind fine:
3 parts dried orange blossoms
1 pt. black peppercorns
1pt. white peppercorns
2 pts. garlic powder
3 pts. roasted dried red chiles (ristras)
2 pts. oregano
2 pts. cumin
1 1/2 pt. orange peel
1 pt. coriander seed
1/2 pt. cinnamon
1 pt. paprika
1/4 pt. clove
1/2 pt. star anise
1/4 pt. thyme
1/2 pt. salt (optional)

Beans, Beans, the Musical Fruit   by joel
    Tunes: Crucifix "Dehumanization"
             Bad Religion anything

Fuck buying canned vegetarian refried/pinto beans. A small can of Rosarita's Vegetarian Refried Beans for 79 cents?!! Fuck that; this recipe costs about 50 cents for a huge potful that tastes ten times better anyway.

Put 2 cups of dry pinto beans in a rather large pot, then fill with water. Adding a spoonful of baking soda at this time helps take out a lot of the "music" to these beans, if you know what I mean. Sprinkle a little cayenne pepper and salt on, and the let soak overnight, or for at least 8 hours or so.

After the beans have soaked, put the pot on the stove and bring to a boil. Turn the heat down to about medium, so that the water is at a slow boil or just below boiling.

Cook the beans for about 2-2 1/2 hours, until nice and soft. Stir occasionally but not too much or else the beans will turn to mush. If the water starts to evaporate, add more. Covering the pot helps decrese evaporation.

As the beans cook, add whatever spices you like. I add salt, black pepper, cayenne pepper, red peppers, chili pepper, and whatever else I'm into at the time. I also like to chop up a medium sized onion and 4-6 roasted chiles and cook them with the beans. At least add the onion; it makes it taste really good. Add whatever vegetables you like; you could probably make an excellent stew with this. Serve piping hot.

If you want to make refried beans, strain the water after the beans are cooked. To make pseudo-refrieds, just blend up the beans until you get a nice mush, then serve. To really RE-fry them, mush them up, put a little oil in a skittle, heat, put the mushed beans in the skillet and cook.

Shampoo

Now what self-respecting vegan doesnt have a lot of hair (Eryc S!@#%&*! excepted, but he's not that self-respecting, anyway)? Now, we all want to take good care of our hair, but we equally despise buying corporate shampoo, with all its chemical additives and long lists of ingredients that we can't pronounce. So, to solve our dilemma, Jacqueline the Master Chef gave us these shampoo recipes, so now you crusties have no excuse not to wash those foul dreads at least once or twice a year.

Jackie's Shampoo for Oily Hair   by Jackie Weltman

2 oz comfrey root (conditioner, thickener)
1 oz yucca root (natural suds, cleans and medicates scalp)
2 oz witch hazel bark (astringent)
1/2 oz lavender flowers (scent, volatile oil)
1 oz nettle leaf (herbal hair tonic)
1/2 oz rosemary leaf (herbal hair tonic)
1 oz yarrow flowers (milfoil, fights oil)

1/2 cup apple cider vinegar (normalizes oil/dry balance)
enough Dr. Bronners peppermint soap to make mild suds

1. Boil the comfrey, yucca and witch hazel in water that covers them with about 1 1/2 inch to spare. Boil at least 30 minutes, covering halfway through. If mixture is still watery, boil until thickened. Strain (DO NOT USE ALUMINUM, FOR BOILING OR STRAINING!).
2. Steep the lavender, nettle, rosemary and yarrow in 3 cups water that was boiling. Let sit for 1 hour to two days (the longer the better). Strain and press out water.
3. Combine solutions and add vinegar and soap.

Shampoo for Blondes or Wannabe Blondes   by Jackie
(Gradually lightens hair)

2 oz comfrey root
1 oz yucca root
2 oz comomile flowers
1 oz rosemary herb
1 oz calendula flower
1/2-1 oz jojoba oil
1/2 cup lemon juice
enough Dr. Bronner's Almond Soap to make mild suds

1. Boil the comfrey and yucca with about 1 inch of water to cover. DO NOT USE ALUMINUM. Boil for at least 30 minutes, covering after 15 minutes to minimize evaporation. If mixture is watery, boil until thicker. Strain.
2. Steep camomile, rosemary and calendula in 3 cups water that has been boiled. Let sit 1 hour to 2 days. Strain.
3. Combine liquids and add oil, lemon juice and soap.

Shampoo for Great Brunette Maintenance   by Jackie
(Gradually darkens hair)

2 oz comfrey root
1 oz yucca root
2oz black walnut hull (green covering of shell)
1 oz rose petals
2 oz rosemary herb
2 oz black walnut leaf
enough Dr. Bronners Almond Soap to make mild suds
1/2 oz jojoba oil (optional)

1. Boil comfrey, yucca and black walnut hull with 1 inch of water to cover. DO NOT USE ALUMINUM. Boil for at least 30 minutes, covering after 15 minutes to prevent evaporation. Strain.
2. Steep rose petals, rosemary and black walnut leaves in 3 cups of boiling water. Let sit for 1 hour to 2 days. Strain.
3. Combine both solutions and add soap, and optional oil and/or aloe.

HIPPYCORE HOMEBREW by joel

Why brew?

Aah, at last we come to the crux, the heart, the very soul of this cookbook--homebrew. I honestly don't think there is a more fulfilling, DIY, punk rock thing you can make than your own beer. Even jack's lasagna or tofu pizza doesn't elicit the complete sense of satisfaction and accomplishment that I feel when I pop open a bottle and take a sip of the most delicious beer that I've tasted and that I made. Brewing your own beer is just too cool, and there's several reasons why.

One, corporate beer sucks. Especially Amerikan corporate beer. Admit it, Bud, Miller, Coors, Pabst, Stroh's, Lucky Lager, whatever, it all tastes like rainwater collected in a spittoon. Not only does corporate beer taste fucking nasty, it's bad business. Nearly every major brewer has its filthy fingers in ugly, exploitative endeavors. Miller Beer (as well as Lite, Miller Geniune Draft, Milwaukee's Best, etc.) is owned by Phillip Morris Company. Not only is Philip Morris a major cigarette manufacturer (Marlboro, etc.), which alone should make you want to stay away from that chamber water, it is also a major campaign contributor to Jesse Helms in North Carolina (that's tobacco country, you know), and the company is generally as racist, reactionary, and wretched as Helms is, supporting the amendment to outlaw flag burning, censoring art and restricting the NEA, supporting the contras, ad nauseum. Face it, Philip Morris and Miller suck, avoid them like the diseased urine they are. (For more shit about Philip Morris, check out A No Record Deal from Pressure Drop Press, POB 460754, SF, CA 94146, $6.)

Coors, despite trying to change their sexist, racist image (for example, they financially support lots of Chicano and Black events and conferences nowadays) and getting the AFL-CIO to call off their "official" boycott, still suck the shit off John Birch's Doc Martens. A family-owned business, folks like Adolf Coors and his relatives were/are members of the John Birch Society, The Heritage Fund (a right wing group that comes out with all these "objective" reports on things like censorship, national defense, etc.), the Council for National Policy (a very right wing, very exclusive group that promotes right wing policies and actions globally), the Moral Majority, and various other scum. They have actively funded the Contras, UNITA forces (a right wing army in Angola, sorta similar to the contras), anti-recycling efforts, etc. Simply put, Coors and their subsidiaries (Coors Light, Henry Weinhardt's, Keystone, Schlitz, Stroh's, etc.) don't deserve what few punk dollars you have, so pass them by. (For more info on Coors write Chale con Coors, POB 8901, Denver, CO 80201 or Earth First!, POB 235, Ely, NV 89301, or see Profane Existence #2.)

I don't know specifically what Anheiser-Busch is up to (anyone got the scoop?), but I've heard stuff about funding contras and other unpunk stuff. Besides, in addition to their sexist ads that sell tits, ass and plastic massified people more than their liquid swill, their beer is the worst-tasting of the lot. Do yourself a favor. Brew your own.

Second, brewing you own beer really pisses off the dogmatic straightedgers. Why? Because 1) It's totally DIY so they can't bitch about how you're supporting death corporations, 2) it's made of totally natural ingredients, so the "alcohol is poison" argument kinda flies out the window, 3) it fucks with the system more than their Nancy Reagan morals do, 4) a sixer of homebrew is cheaper than a $3.50 ep.

Third, homebrew is a great conversation piece at parties. People are genuinely interested in homebrew, and I've gotten more than one person into homebrewing just by sharing a bottle with them. Now that's unity.

Fourth, homebrew is cheap. The initial equipment costs about $50, granted, but once you've made the initial investment one batch of homebrew (five gallons, or about 50+ bottles) costs around $10-12. That's $5-6 a case, and you're lucky to find even Old Milwaukee for that price.

Fifth, homebrew tastes great. It's 100 times better than any amerikan beer, and it rivals European classics, if it doesn't surpass them in flavor and accomplishment (not to mention price), because it tastes that much better because you made it.

Finally, the word I've heard from folks like Jason Bushwhacker, Todd/Pollution Circus, and Tom Scut is that while no animal products are in the ingredients of amerikan corporate swine urine, er, I mean beer, animal products are used in the production of beer. Write to those folks for more info on what's used and why, but if this is true (and I'm sure it is, as these folks are some of the most sussed vegans I know), corporate beer may not even be vegetarian. Get with it, punker. It's time to brew your own.

The Equipment

Making your own beer requires more of an investment than any of the other recipes in this book, financially and temporally. You'll need to buy and scam some equipment, you'll need to put some time into making it. However, the results will be a hundred times worth it. Try to scam as much of this stuff as possible, but be prepared to shell out up to $50 to get you started. For equipment and ingredients, look in the Yellow Pages under "Winemaking Supplies" for a place that sells homebrew equipment in your area. If there's no one near, I'd recommend writing or calling Liberty Malt Supply in Seattle (1432 Western Ave, Seattle, WA 98101, 206-622-1880), as they are cool and knowledgeable people and they do mailorder (I ripped off this recipe from them, too). Okay, you'll need:

-50-100 bottles. The kind that the cap screws off do not work for homebrew. The best kind are longnecks, especially Corona or (gasp) Miller, because their bottles are thick and clear so you can see the color of your masterpiece. Don't use bottles with ceramic caps like Grolsch. It's a good idea in theory, but they don't provide enough pressure and your beer will taste weak if you use them. Trust me. Check the backs of bars for free longnecks, or start drinking and saving.

-One five-gallon plastic bucket with lid. Check out the backs of restaurants or places that sell wallpaper paste, if you don't want to buy one.

-One glass carboy. That's one of those big bluish water cooler bottles. Don't use a plastic one cos the folks at Liberty Malt say they're not good for the beer for some reason.

-One big (1-2 gallon) pot to boil your malt in.

-One siphoning tube. Get one with a nozzle on the end; it helps a lot when you bottle.

-One clamp for the tube.

-One floating thermometer.

-One "fermentation lock." Also called an air lock.

-One bottle capper (wine corkers work great, too).

-A healthy supply of bottle caps

a bag of hops

fermentation lock →

cap

lock →

H₂O to here

cork

into carboy

The Ingredients

There are a million ways to make beer and likewise, there are lots of different kinds of ingredients you can use. I'm just going to tell you how I make Hippycore Homebrew, which is a pretty basic recipe. If you get way into homebrewing, you can buy books on it or write to BURP, which is a zine (yes, a zine) dedicated to the art of homebrewing. I've yet to see a copy myself, but check one out at 19924 Apple Ridge Pl./ Gaittersburg, MD/ 20879). All right, for one batch of Hippycore Homebrew, dark or amber lager, you'll need:

-1 can (53 oz) of unhopped malt syrup. I like John Bull myself. If you want a nice-colored beer that's pretty mellow, try amber. If you want one so dark it makes the coffee those East Bay yahoos drink look like dishwater, try John Bull Dark. It's not bitter or syruppy, either. Personally, it's my favorite.
-1 two ounce bag of boiling hops. I use hallertau hops tied in a bag of cheesecloth, sort of like the teabag principle. Don't use hop pellets, they're cheese.
-1 one ounce bag of finishing hops. I use tetnang in cheesecloth. Once again, fuck pellets.
-1 packet of brewer's yeast. Keep refrigerated until you need it.
-1 1/2-2 cups of corn sugar.

The Method

Making Hippycore Homebrew is a three-step process. From the first boil to the first sip takes 4-6 weeks, depending on your patience, so you should try to always keep one or two batches going to maintain a steady supply.

Step One
Tunes: Poison Idea (of course)
Pleasant Valley Children 7"
Rudimentary Peni "Death Church"

-Wash out your plastic bucket real well. Most folks recommend sterilizing your equipment with bleach, but I'm too lazy.
-Fill your big pot half full of water (if you can get distilled water, great) and start boiling it.
-At the same time, put your can of malt in a saucepan 1/4 filled with water and turn it on a medium heat. This will make the malt syrup less viscous so it will flow out of the can easier, wasting less malt.
-When the water is boiling in the big pot, pour in your malt in and stir constantly. Be sure to be careful that the malt doesn't burn on the bottom of the pot.
-Add your 2oz. bag of boiling hops and boil the mixture (which is called a wort) for 30-60 minutes, the longer the better (sometimes I get lazy). Be sure to stir constantly and always keep an eye on your wort, as this is a sugar mixture and it will boil over very easily. In fact , you'll probably have to pull the pot off the heat a few times to

prevent boilover, especially if you're stuck with a fucking electric stove like me.

-When you decide you're only going to boil your wort for another ten minutes, add your 1 oz bag of finishing hops. Keep stirring.

-At the end of your boil, take the pot off the burner and put the bags in a sieve and pouring hot water over the bags, press out all the liquid in the bags into the wort. We don't want to waste any precious juices now, do we. This is called sparging.

-Put your five gallon plastic bucket in a sink or tub, surround the bucket with ice cold water and put two gallons of cold water inside. Pour in the wort. Add enough cold water to fill the bucket to five gallons.

-Now you'll want to wait until your wort cools to about 65-75 degrees. Drop your floating thermometer in and check it every 15 minutes or so.

-While waiting for the wort to cool, put a teaspoon of corn sugar and a cup of warm water in a ceramic or stainless steel bowl. Add the packet of yeast and cover for 20-30 minutes, allowing the yeast to activate itself a bit (this is also good cos it lets you know if your yeast is a dud before you dump it in your wort).

-When the yeast has risen a bit and the wort has cooled, pitch the yeast, which is homebrew jargon for dumping it in the bucket of wort. Nowe the wort is called the barm.

-Lay the lid on the bucket and place the bucket in a place in your home where the temperature is 65-70. DO NOT PRESS THE LID ON or else you'll have a big mess later; just gently lay it one. If your home is much warmer than 65-70 (like ours in the summer), put it in a tub of water, fill the tub 1" high with water, and wrap a wet towel around it, pouring a cup or two of water on whenever the towel starts to dry. If your home is colder, sit on the bucket like a hen on her eggs. That stuff is gold, Clyde!

Step Two
Tunes: Destroy! demo

-After a day or two, your barm should have gotten really foamy on top.

-After three days, the foam should subside. When it does, siphon the barm into the glass carboy. Leave the greenish, yucky sediment on the bottom of the plastic bucket, but be sure to get as much barm into the carboy as you can (waste not, drink lot). Wash the bucket now before it gets crusty. By the way, the greenish sediment is hops and malt residues and stuff. Don't eat it. Yuck.

-Fill the fermentaton lock halfway with water, then put it into the cork and into the neck of the carboy. Once again, put the barm in a 65-75 degree area.

-Let the barm hang out in the carboy for ten days or so. I don't know why. Just do. Ask your brewer why this step is necessary. I asked once, but I forgot.

Step Three
Tunes: MDC first LP
        Econochrist "Ruination"

-Finally, it's time to bottle. Dissolve 1-1 1/2 cups of corn sugar in a
cup or two of warm water in the plastic bucket. Don't add more than
two cups of corn sugar or you'll end up with a pretty raspy cider, not
beer. Also, the more sugar you add the more fizzy and volatile the
beer, and you don't want too much fizz.
-Siphon the barm from the carboy into the bucket. This is called
priming. Once again, leave the sediment in the carboy, but get out as
much beer as you can. Now you're ready to bottle.
-Siphon the beer into bottles. This is where it comes in real handy to
have a nozzle and clamp setup (see my crude diagram).
-After you've siphoned every last drop into bottles, cap them. Do
yourself a favor and get a good capper, which will cost $10 and up,
but will be well worth it. The cheap kind that you use a hammer
with sucks, and it's easy to bust bottles that way. Wine corkers work
great, as I've said.
-Now, the last and most torturous step. Store your beer in a cool
place (65-70 degrees, again) and wait patiently. This step is called
conditioning, and the longer you condition your beer, the smoother
and tastier it will be. Four weeks is recommended, as it tastes
absolutely primo then, but I often can't wait that long. Give it at
least two weeks.
-Drink up and be fucking stoked. You've fucked the system and
fucked yourself up all in one inexpensive, DIY, and fun swoop.

I know these are a lot of directions, but I wanted to be complete and
make this as user-friendly as possible. Making beer really is a
simple process, and it makes great beer. Remember folks, drinking is
great but drinking your own is euphoria, so get on it!

BREAKFAST FOODS

Banana Flops   by Helium (aka God around Hippycore HQ)

So what kind of a vegan are you, having to read a book to cook
or prepare food! You are a pitiful person. You have been socialized.
You think that 1/2 cup less of this or 1/2 cup more of that will
render your dish inedible. You think that a written recipe is the
optimim balance of the ingredients. . . you are bummed.

Natural foods have the wonderful property of being able to be
blended with each other in any manner or proportion and still
always give a minimum total nutritional value equal to the sum of
their parts, so nutritionally speaking you can't go wrong. Different
combinations will bring different tastes and different textures; a
wonderful array of tastebud experiences that will bring you joyful,
romantic, painful, funny gratifying and humilating memories. . . the
merging of the soul and the pallet.

So my friend, break free from the rigid limit of your food
habits and turn your kitchen into a playground of creativity. . .
Welcome to the BANANA FLOP philosophy.

the training wheels:
around 1 cup of whole wheat flour
around 1/2 cup corn meal
around 3 tablespoons of baking powder
some salt. . . maybe
some soymilk
approximately 3 bananas
around 2 tablespoons of oil (it doesn't matter what kind,
*   goddammit!)*

Here's how I do it:
Mix flour, corn meal, baking powder and some salt. . . maybe,
then add some soy milk and mix well. I like to get the batter as
consistent as. . . well, you know, you'll feel when it's right. Then add
the oil. Chop up the bananas into banana discs or any other shape
you may like and mix them with a small amount of batter in a small
(or big) bowl, just enough so that each piece of banana is covered
with batter.

Now get yourself a cool heavy frying pan and place it on a real
hot surface. Lightly grease the bottom with oil and pour the batter
on the hot fucker. . . yes, it's like pancakes.

While it's cooking place some bananas on top and when you
feel it's the right time, flip it over, or don't flip it at all; it's up to you.
It's all up to you.

Fabulous Fucking French Toast for Freaks
by joel, who ripped it off the back of a Westsoy box.

Okay, this is some really good french toast that doesn't turn out as aesthetically pleasant as the eggy kind, but it's just as delicious nonetheless. It's perfect for those Sunday mornings when the sun is shining through your windows around 10:30 AM and you crawl out of bed yawning and stretching but glad to be awake nevertheless. Open all the windows and doors so you can hear the birds singing outside for this one. This is especially good with a pitcher of orange juice and about 3 or 4 groggy friends.

1 cup soymilk (Westsoy is my choice)
8 oz tofu
a healthy dash of cinnamon
a tad bit of vanilla
half a loaf of good-quality bread--not that Wonder shit. That stuff's
*   not bread, it's fucking cake. Sourdough is preferable here, but*
*   make do with what you have.*
vegetable oil

Dump the soymilk, tofu, cinnamon, and vanilla in a blender and mosh it up to a silky texture. If you don't have a blender, just mash the tofu as best as possible. I've done it this way many times, but the consistency isn't quite as good, but the taste is the same. Put enough oil in a skillet to cover the bottom and heat it up. Put the batter in a bowl and dip a slice of bread in it, covering both sides with the vegan goo. Drop it on the pan and cook for a few minutes, flipping occasionally.

After it's browned on both sides, top it off with vegan margarine and syrup or jam or whatever and eat--you is stoked. This recipe will feed 2-3 folks, so you may want to double it when you've got a hungry touring band staying at your house. Be careful when eating this, though, cos people who do have been known to miraculously start quoting from Sartre or Foucault or Baudelaire, developing an irrisistible urge for a French Bordeaux wine, and begin vehemently insisting that France <u>does</u> have decent hardcore bands.

PUNK Pancakes (j@)

3 cups soy (not oi) milk
4 tablespoons oil
oil for frying
2 teaspoons arrowroot
2 teaspoons water
3 cups flour
2 tablespoons sugar
2 teaspoons baking powder
1/2 teaspoon salt
1 tablespoon cinnamon.

This recipe is great for punks of all ages! Mix the above in a large bowl until it's thick and goopy (like C.O.E. guitar mix). Fry on hot griddle until golden brown (like Eric Scudders tan). Make sure they are relatively thin. When you fry em' wait until you can see holes in the pancakes then flip em' over to get both sides. Yowza!

Waffles   by ???

Okay, so a lot of friends were into waffles and having a hard time getting vegan ones to work out, I came up with this recipe. Ha, we're eatin' 'em today, borrowed the waffle iron from my mom and off we go...

2 1/2 cups unbleached white flour
1 teaspoon vanilla extract (optional)
1/4 cup sweetener (sucarnat (??-ed.))
4 teaspoons baking powder
1 stick margarine-melted
2-3 cups of water

Mix all ingredients, starting with 2 cups of water, adding more water if necessary. Mix well for a few minutes until smooth and elasticy (is that even a word?). It should just be slightly pourable, thick, but pourable.

You can vary this a bit, too. Add date sugar and nuts or coconut and nuts, raisins, berries, etc. Just follow the same recipe

and add whatever yourlike. My favorite topping is soy margarine and rice syrup.

An attempt to define those spiritual principles I try to live by. Ugh.
This one's for you Joel-
VEGANISM

1. Humility and the Principles of non violence.

   In believing that we humans and all that we call "mother earth" is
interconnected vegetarianism is an unavoidable spiritual principle.
As quoted by KRS. one (Boogie Down Productions)-
"I don't eat turkey, chicken, or hamburger, cause to me that's suicide,
self murder". Veganism is the natural progression of this principle.
Factory production of dairy products and eggs is violence and it was
my decision not to support these industries.

2. Economic.

   Many pounds of grain per pound of meat. Rain forests devastated
for the production of meat. As with the other point, it was a natural
conclusion that supporting dairy products eggs and leather was also
denying someone else an opportunity to eat.

3. Support of Alternate Lifestyles.

   Veganism doesn't begin and end at the dinner table. In providing
financial support to co-op groceries and natural food stores you
support the movement as a whole. This also provides a power of
example to those around you in proving it can be done, you won't
starve, and you're better for it.

4. Healthier Diet.

   In making the move to a meatless diet I also made the move
toward a healthier diet. This was also true for the move to veganism.
I was forced to give up on many of the sugar products I was eating
and quit using cheese as my primary source of protein.

5. Most Importantly

_When you hang out with tree hugging vegans like j@ckn' joel you've
got something to talk about! Ha!

Love Timojhen
POB 39638
Rochester NY
14604

Marvelous Mid-day Muffins

This is one of those recipes made for a Sunday afternoon. Birds a singin, 12:40 P.M. Everyone at the HCHQ (more notably Eryc and Steve Styx) asleep.

2 1/2 cups flour
4 tablespoons sugar
5 teaspoons baking powder
1 teaspoon arrow root
1 teaspoon water
1 1/2 cups soy (not oi) milk
2/3 cups vegetable shortening
1 tablespoon cinnamon
1 tablespoon nutmeg

Mix arrowroot and water in a cup and set aside. Put together all dry ingredients in a bowl and add wet ones (and arrow root mix) until you get a nice texture. Grease a baking pan and fill about 2/3 of the way. bake at 400 about 25 minutes or so until light brown. save leftover grease for Jeff Soulforce's hair.

"Rooster's a Crowin'" Brown Rice Corn Cakes with Peanut Sauce   by Jackie Weltman

This is fantastic for breakfast!
2 cups cornmeal
1 cup brown rice flour
1/4 cup vegetable oil
1 teaspoon baking powder
1/4 teaspoon salt
1/4 cup brown sugar or honey (optional)
enough water to make a thick batter

Mix all the ingredients together. Add the water gradually or you'll swim! Pour batter onto hot, greased griddle and cook like pancakes, until brown on both sides. Keep warm in warm oven.

Peanut Sauce
2 cups chunky natural peanut butter (or smooth, if you must)
1 1/4 cup orange juice
1 teaspoon orange rind
1/4 teaspoon cinnamon
2 tablespoon honey

Beat orange juice gradually into peanut butter. Add other ingredients. Cook over moderate heat in saucepan until smooth and slightly thickened. Use a wire whip and stir frequently.
Serve corncakes with peanut sauce, hot!

CAESERS FAVORITE CORNBREAD (j@)

This recipe was apparently used by Caesar in trying to impress the 16 year old Queen Cleopatra. She was so amazed that it contained no animal products she took the recipe back with her to Egypt. In Egypt she gave it to Jun Chan (who was busy at some negotiations) and in turn she gave it to Bart Price who gave it to me.

2 cups flour
6 teaspoons baking powder
1 teaspoon salt
2 cups blue corn meal (yellow is o.k. too)
2 cups soy (never oi) milk
4 teaspoons arrowroot
4 teaspoons water
1/2 cup maple syrup
1/2 cup melted margarine

Combine and mix first four ingredients. Put A. Root in a cup and add water. Pour this mix with the rest and then add soy milk, syrup, and margarine, until it gets real clumpy (like the Roman Army). Put it in a big baking pan (16") at 400 for 20 minutes. Yeah!

J@cknJoel's Diabolical Doughnuts

(This makes tons of em)

2 cups soy (not oi) milk
3 cups sugar
10 cups flour
2 teaspoons salt
1 cup margarine
4 teaspoons arrowroot
4 teaspoons water
1 cup water
4 tablespoons cinnamon
4 teaspoons ground nutmeg
oil for frying
powdered sugar

First of all you won't find vegan doughnuts at Dunkins or Winchells but you will find them at the HC house on a Sunday afternoon. Mix all the above ingredients (arrow root and drops of water separately, then add) Get yer' hands in there and mush it up! (Bro). Now fry them in oil. Make sure they are small and thin and subsumed in the oil. (Otherwise they come out gooey). After they look nice n' brown on both sides put them on a paper towel to get some grease off. Pour some powdered sugar in a bag- while doughnuts are semi-hot throw them in there and shake em' up, oooh-oooh shake em' up. Serve with pink lemonade and a huge smile!

LUNCHES/QUICK FIX FOODS

Howdy-Ho Sloppy Joels   by joel
Tuneage: Desecration live tapes
                Amebix "Arise"

This is great for a quick meal that tastes pretty fucking good. It's also perfect for feeding touring bands and whatnot. Jack and I like to eat this while bitching about the system.

1 can of S&W Chili beans (believe me, no other brand is quite the same)
Nature's burger (1 part nature's burger to 1 pt. boiling water)
onions
bread
ketchup and mustard (mostly mustard)
chili pepper, cayenne pepper, red pepper

Boil some water for your nature's burger. Mix the water and burger mix (1:1 ratio, approximately) and shape into lovely heart-shaped patties (I'm feeling a bit romantic right now). Fry up the nature's bruger with a little oil in a frying pan as you would a hamburger in your less compassionate days, sprinkling in a little garlic salt as you go. If you're feeling really rebellious, slap a slab of tofu in the pan and cook that, too. While this is cooking, heat up yer beans and chop up your onions. S&W beans are great but they're not nearly spicy enough, so mix in healthy doses of chili, cayenne and red pepper. If your eyes well up with tears, it's probably spicy enough. I hope you tossed some bread in the toaster by now, else you'll have to eat it cold. Put the bread on a plate. Place the nature's burger (and tofu, if you cooked some) on top, and then smother the lot with beans, beans, beans. Sprinkle onions and squirt mustard and ketchup over the whole mess, grab a fork and chow! The flatulence quotient of this recipe is fairly high, so this is good revenge food to eat when your roommates are being wise asses.

Tofu Burgers   by Donna Rivest

1 1/2 cup tofu, crumbled
1/2 cup chopped onion
1 minced garlic clove
1/2 teaspoon basil
1/2 teaspoon oregano
1/8 teaspoon pepper
1 1/2 cup cooked rice or bulgur (or a combo of both)
1/2 cup bread crumbs

Combine tofu and herbs. Mix well. Stir in rice or bulgur. Stir in bread crumbs. Form into patties and fry in oil.

Dagwood Bumstead's Favorite Sandwich   by joel
Tunes: Cringer, anything
Dead Silence, anything

Betcha' didn't know ol' Dagwood was a vegan, didja? Well, he is. He pretends to eat meat and cheese cos the stupid cartoonist draws him that way, but behind the panels it's strictly cruelty free for our good Mr. Bumstead. Anyway, he gave me this recipe a few years ago, and I still worship it to this day.

Submarine rolls or bread; sourdough tastes best
Nature's burger
tofu
lettuce, tomato, sprouts, onions, mushrooms, chopped
mustard and ketchup

Spread vegan margarine on the bread and grill it on a griddle at low heat. Boil some water for the nature's burger, too, and while that's going, cut up your vegetables. When the water's boiling, mix it with your Nature's burger (1:1 ratio). Form the burger into a nice patty about 1/4-1/2 inch thick in the shape of your bread. Put a bit of oil in a frying pan and when the oil is hot, plop in your "burger" patty. Also, cut a 1/4" slice of tofu from the block and put that into the pan, too. If you're into grilled onions and mushrooms like our pal Daggie, this is the time to throw 'em in the frying pan and cook them as well. Spice the whole mess up with a little garlic salt and

nutritional yeast and flip tofu and burger occasionally. Cook until tofu and patty are well-browned, then slap both on the grilled bread and pile the mushrooms and onions on top. Add your (Martin) sprouts, lettuce, tomatoes, ketchup, mustard, and the kitchen sink. Place the other piece of bread on top like a crown jewel. Now, the challenge is to fit this delightful whopper into your big mouth, but I'm sure you'll have a good time trying. Great with potoato chips and Jack's peanut butter chocolate chip cookies.

Pandora's Pasta Salad

This one won't release any evils into the world but it will release a very pleasing taste to your tummy.

```
1/2  head  romaine  lettuce
8 oz. rotini (or any pasta you dig, I like curly ones)
3  tomatoes,  diced
2  15 oz. cans kidney, beans
2  bell  peppers
1/2  red  onion
5 oz. oil
6 oz. red wine vinegar
2 tablespoons garlic salt
 "      "         oregano
1      "         basil
 "      "            cayenne pepper
 "      "            black pepper
```

Start boiling water and cook rotini for about 20 minutes. Mix vinegar and oil and set aside. Cut up all veggies and put in large mixing bowl. Add pasta when it's cooked and add a bit of oil and vinegar at a time with spices. Mix! Add more spices as you go until all is used. If it ain't spicy enough don't be afraid to put more in. Refrigerate for at least 30 minutes and as soon as you can unleash this delicious box of delicacies.

Syrian Green Beans   by Kamala

```
1  medium-sized  onion
olive oil
1 lb. green beans, cut into bite-sized pieces
4 tablespoons tomato sauce

1 1/4 cups water
salt and pepper
dash of allspice (ground)
dash of mint leaves (fresh or dried)
lavash or pita bread
soy butter
```

Brown onion in a medium-sized pan with enough olive oil to coat bottom of pan. Stir in green beans, then add tomato sauce. Stir well and add the water. Add salt, pepper, allspice and mint. Bring to a boil. Reduce heat and cover. Simmer for about 30 minutes or until beans are tender. Eat with plenty of bread and butter.

Grilled Corn-on-the-Cob   by Donna Rivest

Peel the husks of the corn back as far as possible, making sure that the husks aren't completely removed. Remove silk from ears, then carefully fold husks back in place, covering entire cob.

Soak ears in ice water for 30 minutes. When the corn soaks in ice water, the kernels soak up the water. That way when the corn is grilled, the kernels steam themselves.

Grill over low heat, leaving husks on the corn, for approximately 30 minutes. It's okay if the husks burn; the corn won't if properly covered by the husk.

Bettina's Noodles With Beans   by Bettina Turek

Cook some long thin noodles in water for about ten minutes. Put a can of white beans in a pot and saute with a little margarine.

Get another saucepan for the sauce. Put 3 tablespoons margarine in the pan and melt it. Add 2 tablespoons flour and stir fast. Add a cup of water or soy milk, as well as any spices you want.

Put the noodles with the beans in a pot, and pour sauce over all.

Baked Apples   by Bastian Buchmeier

Hollow out some apples. Fill them with almond paste, raisins, almonds, hazel nuts and marmelade. Wrap the apples in tin foil and then bake them in the oven at around 300-350 degrees.

"Ox" Lentil Paste   by Joachim Hiller

100 grams (approx. 1/2 cup) lentils (any kind)
1 carrot, chopped
1 bunch scallions, chopped
1/2 cube of bouillion
1 little onion, chopped
150 grams margarine
salt, pepper, marjoram

Put lentils in water for 2-3 hours. Boil lentils, carrots and scallions. Sauté the onions. Slightly heat the margarine, then put everything in a mixer and mix it real good. Add salt, pepper and marjoram. Put in the fridge to chill. It will keep for about a week, or you can freeze it.

Middle Eastern Yummies   by Naomi Green

All the main ingredients for these three recipes are premixed, uh, mixes. You can buy them at your local health food store or co-op. You can always find them in cute little boxes with nice labels and not much content, or if your store is cool, you'll be able to find them in bulk packages, which is better to buy economically and environmentally.

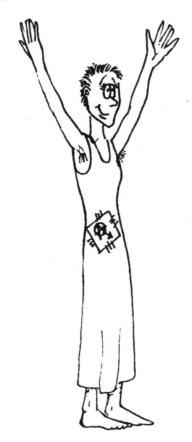

Tabouli Salad

1 cup tabouli mix
1 cup water
1/3 cup olive oil
chopped tomatoes, cucumbers, onions (as much as you want)

Mix it all together and let it sit for about an hour in the refrigerator--mixing occasionally. Ta Da! It's done and ready to be chomped.

Cous Cous

1 cup cous cous (a neat-o grain)
2 1/2 cups water
handful of raisins or currants (optional but yummy)

Put the water on to boil in a covered pot. When the water reaches a laughing boil, toss in the cous cous. Uncover and turn down the flame. Drop in the raisins and stir. This cooks a lot like rice only real fast. In 5-10 minutes the cous cous has sucked up all the water and is ready.

To eat a main meal, you can toss in some chopped veggies when you first put the water on. Fast, easy, and yummy.

You Won't Feel Awful About This Falafel

1 cup falafel mix
water
. pita bread
tomatoes peppers, cucumbers, mint, chopped
1 cup tahini (sesame butter)
3/4 cup lemon juice
lots of minced garlic

Mix up the falafel mix with boiled water until it has an oatmeal-like consistency. Let it sit in the refrigerator for an hour or until it is more solid (this step is optional).

When the mix is ready, heat about 2 cups of vegetable oil in a deep frying pan. This is the tricky part; if the oil gets too hot it starts to fill the room with smoke (as we found out at the Hippycore House). However, the oil has to be hot enough to deep fry those falafels. Spoon up the mix just like you're making cookies, flatten into little patties, and drop into the hot oil. A slotted spoon or a pair of tongs is best for this maneuver. Cook until brown, and watch for splattering oil!

Now, throw 2 cute little cooked falafel patties in 1/2 a pita pocket with the chopped up veggies.

To get really fancy you can try out the sauce. Mix up the tahini, lemon juice, and garlic. Tahini is hard to stir, but work with it a little; it's fun. The sauce will be real thick, just right to smear on falafels. You may want to smear this inside the bread before you stuff it with falafels and vegetables.

So, if you make all this stuff, you'll have a hip mideastern meal. Feed it to all your friends. It's a good meal for carnivores interested in a better way of eating.

Why Todd/Pollution Circus is a Vegan

I'm a vegan because I cannot support the exploitation of any creature; it goes against one of the main aspects of my belief system as an anarchist, that of freedom and liberation. For me, freedom/ liberation cannot be only for one species, it must be for all , otherwise freedom would be a farce. I learned slowly in my life of the exploitation of other creatures, and as I became aware I found I could not support it; my conscience would not let me. It started out quite early with obvious things: meat, fish, poultry. Then, as I found out about such things as vivisection and dairy "farming", I gave up more and more things. I've since become quite strict as to what I will consume or use.

I do not see veganism as a sacrifice of any sort; I see it as an embracing of a more compassionate and environmentally sound way of living. And yet, I don't live with blinders on; I see it also goes a lot further than just personal veganism. It also brings a yearning for change, largescale change, in the view of other species and this planet we live on. I realize that we can strive to be "pure" vegans, but we cannot be as "pure" as we would like.

We can only do our best to avoid what we can; byproducts are everywhere, in plastics, paper, metal manufacturing, cement, in the processing of foods like sugar, vinegar, and alcohol (yes, even beer, wine, liquor). They're in many, many places we'd never imagine, but then just imagine the unbelievable numbers of animals murdered daily throughout the world, and all the waste/byproducts produced. They all go somewhere, and it all goes to show the need for change is great and the time to change is now, in how we treat each other and the other animals on this planet and the planet itself. When it all comes down to it I guess I'm a vegan because I'm a lover of life and of freedom, for myself and all others.

Fry Bread   by Todd/Pollution Circus

2 cups unbleached, unenriched white flour
1/2 teaspoon baking soda
1 teaspoon salt
enough water to make a soft dough that holds itself together

Knead until elasticity starts, approximately 3-5 minutes. Tear off small balls of dough and roll out to about 1/4 inch thickness (you can do it with your hands instead of a pin) and fry in hot oil. Kind of deep fry, about 1/4 inch of oil in the pan. Fry on both sides till golden brown.

For "Indian Tacos," top with beans, tofu, lettuce, avocado, tomato, sprouts, etc.

For blue corn frybread substitute 2/3 cup of blue corn flour for 2/3 of the white flour (i.e. 2/3 blue corn flour, 1 1/3 cups white flour). Blue corn frybread can also be made sweet and it's wonderful. Add 1-2 tablespoons of the sweetener of your choice (I use rice syrup or "sun evap. cane juice") to the dough and top with cinnamon and rice syrup or fruits and nuts.

For "Indian Pizza" top with salsa and sauted or steamed tofu and vegetables.

"Isle of Lesbos" Stuffed Grape Leaves   by Empress Jackie W.

1 bottle grape leaves in brine (available at natural or gourmet shops)
3 cups cooked brown rice
1/2 cup lemon juice (or more or less to taste)
several tablespoons chopped fresh dill (approx. 1/4 cup)
1 tablespoon white wine vinegar
1/2 cup chopped pinenuts, NOT toasted
1/2 cup + 3 tablespoons olive oil (or more to taste)
several tablespoons chopped fresh mint (at least 2)
2 teaspoons cracked black pepper
1/2 cup dried currants (optional)
salt to taste

Combine the brown rice, cooked, with the lemon juice, vinegar, olive oil, herbs, pinenuts, pepper and currants. Mix well. Mound about one tablespoon in the center of a grape leaf, toward the stem. Next, start rolling it up from the stem end. As you get to just before the middle, tuck in the sides, then finish the roll and place seam side down *(see intricate illustrations)*. Basically, it's rolled like a burrito. Some folks say steam these to soften, but I think they're great raw-- crunchy outside. If you want to steam them, place them in a frying pan with a <u>thin</u> layer of water and cover and heat at low heat till soft.

Pasta al Chaos   **by Tom Messmer**

bunch of broccoli
large clove(s) of garlic
several mushrooms
1/2 lb. of pasta
1/4-1/2 cup olive oil
salt
pepper
oregano
basil

First, take a dirty pot and a dirty frying pan out of the pile in the sink. Wash them. Boil a good amount of wa wa. While waiting for water to boil, remember you still have to cook the vegetables. Frantically rummage through the dirties until you find a medium sized pan and a veggie steamer. Steam vegetables (chop them first!). Smash garlic with the flat of knife blade then chop into small bits (that's mince to us pros). Pour olive oil in frying pan and add garlic, oregano and basil. Don't turn the heat on yet. Add pasta to water (this should be done at the same time the veggies are added to steam). When pasta and veggies are nearing completion, turn heat on and saute garlic and spices in oil for no more than 2 minutes. Strain pasta and add to frying pan. Add vegetables along with some of the water they were cooking in. Toss. Eat directly out of frying pan.

MAIN DISHES

Barley Soup/Stew   by Michael/Ireland

1 cup pot barley
1 large onion, chopped
3 large potatoes, chopped
3 large carrots, chopped (or other root vegetable)
1 teaspoon yeast extract or vegetable stock
1/2 teaspoon thyme
1 teaspoon miso
a little tamari (soy sauce)
a little sea salt

First, put the barley into a heavy saucepan with 3 cups of water and a little salt. Boil and then simmer on a very low heat for about 1 hour, by which time all the water will have been absorbed. Meanwhile, chop the potatoes and carrots and put them in a different pot with the yeast extract with about 1 pint of water, or else put in 1 pint of vegetable stock. Boil and simmer for about 10-15 minutes, until soft, then add the chopped onion and the thyme and some tamari, if desired. Add the cooked barley and let simmer for another 15-20 minutes. Add more water if it is too thick, then remove from the heat. Dissolve the miso in a small amount of the soup and then add to the pot--don't cook anymore or the beneficial enzyme in the miso will be destroyed.

The soup does taste good without the miso, but it adds a real nice flavor to include it. Great for cold winter days!

Tomato-Barley Soup   by Donna Rivest

2/3 cup barley
4 cups vegetable stock or water
1 tablespoon margarine or oil
2 minced garlic cloves
1 chopped onion
4 chopped carrots
2 chopped celery stalks
3 cups cooked tomatoes
3/4 cup tomato paste
2 tablespoons dried parsley
1 teaspoon each of thyme, dill, marjoram, tarragon
pepper to taste

Combine barley and stock in a large pot. Saute garlic and onion in margarine. Add to stock. Stir in carrots, celery and tomatoes. Simmer 1 hour. Stir in tomato paste and herbs. Flavor with pepper.

Jackie's Famous Green Gazpacho (Soup)   by Jackie Weltman

10 cucumbers, peeled and seeded
10 tomatillos
10 cloves garlic
2 onions, medium
2 green peppers, seeded
1 bunch fresh cilantro
1-2 serrano or jalapeño chiles
1/4-1/2 cup lime juice, to taste
2 tablespoons mint, fresh
salt to taste

Add fresh tomatillos to rapidly boiling water and boil 3 minutes or until soft. Remove husks. Combine tomatillos with all vegetables and herbs and purée in blender or processor. Stir in lime juice and salt to taste. It works better to mince the peppers and garlic and dice other veggies before puréeing. Serve cold.

Why I'm Vegan
by Eryc S@#%$&*!

It was a cool summer's evening in San Francisco when I made the big decision. Looking back, it doesn't seem like such a big deal; it just makes eating out and shopping a big pain in the ass. I had been lacto-ovo vegetarian for two years prior to veganizing, something that was sparked by my interest in animal rights. I won't bore you (unless it's too late for that) with the gory and redundant details of how much pain and torture factory farm animals must endure for your burger and milkshake. Seeing the pictures and reading the pamphlets stopped me from eating animals, but the milk, eggs, cheese, etc. didn't go out the window until it finally hit me how heavily our lifestyles revolve around the "cultivation" of animals. It took me a long time to work up the willpower to get to the point where I finally said, "NO, I'M NOT GOING TO DO IT ANYMORE." After that, it was a breeze. Of course, I would have never gotten to the point that I have without the influence of my friends. I guess I just realized that you don't have to try and save the world, since it may be too late for that. But at least I can say I didn't take part. Don't get me wrong, I don't think being vegan makes me better than anyone, but it's one less thing on my conscience, and a lot less blood on my face.

J@CK N' ERYC's HOT AND SPICY CHINESE SOUP

(This is called Jack n' Eryc's cuz' Eryc was there when I made it- j@)

1/2 head cabbage
1 onion
1 bunch scallions (green onions dummy)
3 carrots
1 block tofu
 1 cup soy (need I repeat not oi) sauce
2 tablespoons Oregano
                   Ginger
                   Cumin
                    Black Pepper

5 tablespoons corn starch
5 tablespoons water

    Put all veggies in a pot of boiling water. Add soy (not oi) sauce until the broth becomes a beautiful brown color. Next add spices and tofu. Let simmer (not S$#%^&(^%$) for about 20 minutes or so. It is hot and damn good.

Minestrone Alla Genovese **by Rossana**

4 quarts water
2 cups potatoes, diced
2 cups celery, sliced
4 small zucchini, sliced in 1/2 inch pieces
about 1 1/2 cups sliced leeks
1 pound Italian (Romano) green beans, cut in 2-3 inch lengths
1/2 cup salad macaroni (ditalini)
1 pound peas, shelled
3-4 cups shredded white cabbage
about 2 teaspoons salt
pesto sauce

Bring water to boil and add potatoes. Cover and simmer 10 minutes. Remove cover and add celery, zucchini, leeks, green beans, and macaroni and simmer 5 minutes. Stir in peas and cabbage and cook 4-5 minutes more.

Ladle soup at once into bowls and spoon in pesto sauce to taste.

Basic Potato Stew **by joel**

Cooking Jams: Offspring Lp
                FUAL Lp

This one's basic cos it's simple, not as spicy as most of my recipes, and hearty. You'll need:

a large pot
fill it halfway with potatoes, largely diced
4-6 carrots
3-4 stalks o' celery
1 or 2 bunches of green onions
1 regular onion
1/2 head of cabbage
1/2 stick vegan margarine
3-4 big spoonfuls of flour
spices like black pepper, garlic salt, garlic powder (or dice up 1
*   clove), cayenne pepper, basil, oregano, etc.*
anything else you like that's lying in the fridge-experiment!

Fill the pot that's half full of potatoes 3/4 full of water, spice it up, and then set it on the stove and start boilin'. While this is cooking, dice up the rest of the veggies fairly large (this is a stew, remember). When you've done that, dump 'em in the pot, add more spices, and cook for a while, until all the veggies are soft (especially the carrots and potatoes). When things are progressing nicely, put another record on and then go back to the stove. In a small saucepan, melt a half stick of margarine. When that's melted, add spoonful by spoonful the flour and scramble rapidly so the mixture doesn't burn. You're making what is called a roux (roo, as in croo-sin' or "Fruck roo" when you have a large piece of cotton in your mouth), and it's a great substance, excellent for thickening up almost any soup or sauce. Add flour to your roux until you get a dry, pasty substance. You want it to be more of a solid than a liquid mixture. Cook the roux for a couple minutes, stirring con-stantly. When your veggies taste done, scoop the roux in the pot spoonful by spoonful, stirring the soup constantly as you go along. You should notice the stew start to thicken almost immediately. Add roux until you get a consistency that you like, and save the leftover roux for another time (it lasts forever). Stir, simmer for a while, and taste. Add whatever spices you feel necessary. This would taste great with homemade noodles, but I don't know how to make them, yet. Another suggestion would be to serve hot homemade biscuits with it (see recipe elsewhere). Minimally, eat with a fistful of crackers (not metal, sorry Jack). EEE-Yummy! as my dad would say. This stew is guaranteed to warm the cockles of your heart, even those crusty punks who are crazy enough to live in frigid Minneapolis (hi Troll).

Chick Pea Somosas   by Christy Colcord

Pastry:
4 oz wholemeal flour
1/2 oz melted margerine
3-4 fluid oz cold water (1/2 cup)

Filling:
2 oz chick peas (garbanzo beans) or 4 oz canned ones
1 small onion, very finely chopped
1 clove garlic, minced
2 small carrots, very finely diced
1 medium potato, very finely diced
4 oz cauliflower, broken into small pieces
2 oz fresh or frozen peas
1/2 vegetable stock cube or 1/2 teaspoon stock concentrate
1 tablespoon oil or vegan margarine for frying
1/2 teaspoon cayenne powder
1 teaspoon curry powder
1 teaspoon wholegrain mustard
1 teaspoon turmeric
1 teaspoon cumin
1 teaspoon coriander
1 teaspoon garam masala (optional)
oil for deep frying

Make the filling first. Presoak and cook chick peas. Drain and save liquid.

Fry the onion, garlic, carrot, potato, cauliflower, and peas in the oil or margarine until softening. Add the cayenne, curry, mustard, turmeric, cumin, and coriander and fry for another couple minutes, stirring constantly. Add the stock cube and 1/4 pint of the saved chick pea liquid. Bring to a boil, then lower heat. Cover and simmer for 10-15 minutes, until the vegetables are soft and all the liquid is absorbed.

Add the cooked chick peas and garam masala. Stir well, then allow to cool while you make the pastry (you may want to even put it in the freezer).

To make the pastry, mix the flour and melted margarine, then add enough cold water to make a smooth, non-sticky dough that leaves the sides of the bowl clean. Knead the dough well until it is smooth and elastic and divide into 6 small balls the size of a walnut. Roll out each ball on a floured board to a thin saucer-sized circle.

Make it as thin as possible. Cut each circle in half to for12 semicircles. Put one big spoonful of <u>cold</u> filling on each semicircle of pastry. The filling has to be cold and relatively not wet to work or the pastry will be soggy and you'll be fucked.

Brush the edges with water, then fold the pastry over the filling and seal the edges well by pinching together to form 12 triangular things.

Heat some oil in a wok or deep pan until almost smoking. Deep fry the samosas a few at a time for about 5 minutes, until they are puffed out and crispy brown. Drain on absorbent paper and serve immediately, allowing 3 per person or more because they're great. I also think they're just as good cold for lunch--the spices soak in.

Store leftovers in fridge. They'll keep for about 3 days. You can reheat them in the oven for about 15 minutes at about 350 degrees.

Note: they're better frozen before fried. It takes awhile to make these the first couple of times, but once you get the hang of it, it goes pretty fast. Man is it worth it--these things are so great it's unbelievable! *(Editor's note: We here at the Hippycore Kitchen can only agree with Christy in the strongest possible terms. Try this recipe; somosas absolutely fucking rule!)*

Veg Sushi   by Jun

Rice
Water to steam--one inch above rice level
Vinegar for ten cups of rice: one cup vinegar
4 tablespoons of sugar
1 tablespoon salt
Some sheets of seaweed. If you can't get them anywhere, use lettuce or spinach leaves
wasabi (Japanese green mustard)
cucumber
celery
takuan (Japanese pickles)
soy sauce

Steam rice. Add vinegar, sugar and salt in the steamed rice. cut vegetables into strips. Tear seaweed into four squares. Spread rice on seaweed or lettuce leaves. Put Wasabi on as desired and add vegetables. Roll them up and put soy sauce on top.

Indian Vegetable Stew   by Melanie Boyd

5 large cooking tomatoes, quartered
1 large eggplant, cubed
roughly 200g (approx. 8 oz) tofu
3-4 potatoes, cubed
1/2 tablespoon ginger
1/2 teaspoon chile powder
1 1/2 teaspoons black mustard seeds
1/4 teaspoon asafetida (hing)
pinch of turmeric
1 teaspoon garam masala
2 teaspoons salt

Break or cut tofu into rough 1/2 inch cubes and deep-fry in oil until golden.

Put tomatoes in covered pot with 1/2 cup water. Simmer for 15 minutes and strain to romove skins and hard bits.

Deep-fry or parboil the eggplant and potato cubes.

Fry ginger, chile, mustard seeds and asafetida in the bottom of a large pot until the seeds start popping. Add the tomato pureé and vegetables, salt, and remaining spices. Simmer for 8 minutes, then add tofu and cook for 2 more minutes.

Warzone's "Mexican" Bean Stew   lifted by Gert in Dublin

1 1/2 cups green lentils
2 green bell peppers
10 oz kidney beans
handful of mushrooms
2 tablespoons tomato puree
2 diced carrots
3 potatoes, diced
1/2 pint water
1 1/2 teaspoon chili powder
2 teaspoon cumin
pepper and salt

Rinse and boil the lentils for 40 minutes. Fry vegetables and spices in a little oil in a pot. Add water and simmer for 20 minutes. Add cooked lentils and puree and salt and pepper and simmer for 10 more minutes. Voila. It's really nice--really!

Chaos Crust Tofu Chili   by Troll

1 pound fresh tofu
1 pound dried red kidney beans
4 tablespoons chili powder
1 hot chili pepper (finely chopped--seeds removed for the meek)
1 medium-size yellow squash or medium zucchini, chopped small
2 onions, coarsely chopped
1 green bell pepper, chopped
2 8 ounce cans of tomato paste
1/2 cup brown rice

Okay, you have to plan ahead a little bit for this one, now. On the night before you plan on eating this, put the tofu in the freezer (trust me, it gives it a firmer texture when re-thawed) and put the kidney beans in a pot with about 6-8 cups of water and let soak over night. About one hour before you plan on eating, put the pot with the beans on the stove over a medium heat and toss your frozen tofu (ice water and all) into the pot, as well as all of the rest of the ingredients, except the zucchini or squash. Bring to a boil and then let simmer for one hour. You may need to add some water along the way and remember to stir every 5 minutes or so or else you will burn your chili. After an hour, the beans and brown rice should be sufficiently cooked; if not, continue to simmer. When beans and rice are cooked (tender), add zucchini or squash and cook for five more minutes, then serve. Some other vegetables you may want to use may be broccoli, cauliflower, carrots (they take longer to cook), corn, etc. You may also want to add black pepper or tobasco sauce for more bite.

To be perfectly honest, I was drawn into being a vegetarian, and then a vegan, through involvement in the punk rock community. That may seem utterly trite to some people who are new to the punk rock "scene", but I'm proud of the fact and to me this is just another shining example of how involvement in such a movement has changed my lifestyle and that of many others for the better.

When I first got involved in punk rock an unimportant number of years ago, I had visions of it being comprised of disenchanted whiz-kids who hated being mainstream. In a way I was right and met a lot of people I consider very intelligent but with no desire to do what society, peer-pressure and consumer marketing wanted them to do. Unfortunately, as was my case as well, most of these people took out their frustrations with society in a generally self-destructive manner. I've seen all too many incredibly intelligent, free-thinking people destroy themselves through drugs, reckless suicidal activity, or just succumbing in one way or another to modern society, like becoming yuppies.

I consider myself lucky enough to instead form an attitude completely opposite. To me, punk rock was more of a community of people looking to each other for help, respect and friendship. When I first seriously looked into the ideals of anarchism, it seemed that this was an idea that was right for me. My distaste for society was already there, and anarchism became a vision I too shared. This reinforced my desire for building an alternative lifestyle based on love and mutual respect. Needless to say, I've made it my foremost goal to put the ideals of anarchism into work in every aspect of my life.

When confronted with the ideas of animal rights, I quickly took them into favor. The idea of respect for all sentient creatures, not just human life, fit all too well with my outlook on life. My transition from being a meat-eater to being a vegan was only slowed by my limited knowledge in the area, but I credit the punk rock movement fully for this. I'm very much proud that this movement has changed me in this way and am likewise equally proud to be involved with it. I think a lot of credit needs to be given to Joel and Jack for putting this together, as well as the others who are taking part. I know that if it weren't for dedicated people like them, I would not be here contributing today.

--Troll/Profane Existence

"Oh shit, I'd better cook the vegetables before they turn rotten!" Stew by joel

Tunes: Whatever band is practicing in my living room at the moment.

You know the story. You go shopping and buy a cartful of vegetables, planning to cook up a veritable cornucopia of vegetable dishes for the next week. However, things never work out that way, do they. You're too tired to cook one night, you go out for Mexican food the next night and then to your parents for free grub the following day, and before you know it there's a pungent odor seeping through the refrigerator doors. The mushrooms are blackening, the tomatoes and bell peppers are getting squishy, a hint of mold is

appearing on the cauliflower, and yucky white roots are starting to pop out of the eyes of your potatoes. You need to take action and fast. Here's how I do it:

oil
potatoes are pretty much a staple, though not irreplaceable
any veggies that are about to go icky
a big can of tomato paste
a can of beans, if there's one around
tofu, if you have it (or tempeh)
lots of spices, whatever you're into, but especially black pepper

In a big pot, put a thin layer of oil. Dice up your potatoes and onions and anything else that's solid in texture and throw it in the pot of hot oil (just like the Christians used to do to infidels). If you're adding any slightly smelly tofu, this is the time to do it. Let this cook for a while, dumping in lotsa spices. This time I added pepper (lots), curry powder (lots), cumin, cayenne pepper, garlic salt, garlic powder, oregano, lemon pepper, you know, the usual. While this is cooking, chop up all the veggies in your fridge that are going bad (I cut out the moldy and squishy parts, but the more adventurous of you will want to retain them for flavor). Toss 'em in when the potatoes seem about half done and cook this on high heat for a few minutes. Then, add a big can of tomato paste (sauce, puree, whatever) and a can of beans (kidney or pinto, preferably), more spices, and stir.

Cook on high for a few minutes, then put on low heat, cover, and let simmer for 15-20 minutes, until the potaotoes are soft (or you're too hungry to wait any longer). Serve with crackers and whatever other nonspoilable dry goods you have, and praise yourself for salvaging the veggies from being wasted and for avoiding a nasty case of food poisoning to boot.

Joel's Devil Chili

3 cans kidney beans
2 cans peeled tomatoes and a bunch of real ones
1 16 oz. block tofu
a good amt. of natures burger
lotsa veggies: corn on the cob, onions, chives, green bell peppers,
zucchini, etc..   whatever is in the fridge basically
lotsa spices: my favorite are the three c's (Curry, Cumin, and
Coriander) chili powder, Cayenne Pepper, lemon pepper, dried red
peppers, black pepper, garlic, and basil leaves (phew!)
whatever you put in, the word is SPICY.

    Like almost everything I cook, this comes out different every time, depending on my need, what's in the fridge, how many I'm cooking for etc... So like most of my recipes, treat this as a rough sketch and develop your own chili. Remember, cooking is fun!

    Allright, in the biggest pot you have, put in the beans, tomatoes, and a healthy dash of all the spices. Turn it on medium to low heat, stirring occasionally, while this is cooking dice up the tofu and fry it in a pan with some oil. Add a dash of garlic salt and curry powder so the tofu will soak up the flavor. Cook this up for about 5-7 minutes and when it tastes done and feels firm dump it in the pot. Keep the heat on and add a bit more oil and dump in the big bowl of veggies you should have been chopping while grooving to the SAINTS. Fry it till the veggies are pretty cooked but still crispy and dump em' in too. Follow this up with a 2nd dashing of all spices.

    O.K. now here's my secret. While the tofu is frying, boil a small pot of water. Mix the water with some natures burher (about 50/50 mix is good) While the veggies are in the frying pan crumble the natures burger into chunks and fry them in a separate pan. Things can get hectic here, with three things on the stove at once, but it's worth it, believe me, besides your tough.

    When the natures burger is cooked to your liking dump it in the pot which by now should be so thick you can eat it with a fork. Taste it to see if it's spicy enough, if it doesn't make your nose run, add more.

    After it's all spiced up let it cook on low for a few minutes so the various flavors can meld together then serve it with soda crackers and homebrew. Deelicious! Even hardcore carnivores NOFX had to admit this chili kicks some serious ass. Feeds 5-8 folks or 2 people for 4 days, YEAH!

Cholent   (Jewish stew)   by Donna Rivest

2 cups pinto beans, cooked
1 tablespoon oil
2 garlic cloves, minced
1 cup onion, chopped
5 cups water
2 cubes vegetable boullion
1/2 cup barley
1 potato, diced
2 teaspoons paprika

Saute onion and garlic in oil. Boil water and boullion. Add beans, onion, barley, potato, paprika. Stir. Bring to another boil, then reduce heat, cover and simmer for 2 hours.

Potato and Nature's Burger Dish   by   Jennifer Stratman

olive oil, or any other vegetable oil in your cupboard
3-4 potatoes
1-2 onions, depending on how well you like them
10 or more mushrooms
a good handful of snow peas
a few cloves of garlic
1/2 box of Nature's Burger, or any meat substitute
tofu, if you have some
tortillas
curry powder
seasoned pepper
basil
garlic powder (spices are optional, of course, but they do add flavor)
any other vegetable going rotten in your fridge that might sound
*   good*
a skillet with a lid and a spatula

First, prepare Nature's Burger (1:1 ratio to hot water and stir). While you're letting it cool, cut up the veggies. Next, oil your skillet and turn on burner to the mark in between medium and medium high. Toss in potatoes and onions and tofu first. Then, in a couple minutes, toss in the rest of the veggies and Nature's Burger. Spice to your own taste and cover the skillet. When the potatoes are soft you know it's done. Roll it up in a tortilla and eat.

Punk-Wok Stirfry   by joel

Wokin' tunes: Beatnigs LP
                Night Soil Man LP

rice (a nice big potful)
lotsa veggies
tofu (one block)
lotsa spices
oil

Yeah, I know you're sick of those wok puns, but tough shit. Anyway, this is a really loose recipe that is practically guaranteed come out tasting great, so just follow the rough outline of this recip (and most of the other ones I write, too, for that matter) and experiment with it and have fun.

First off, start cooking some rice.   Scratch that; first make sur you have some homebrews chilling in the fridge. Okay, now that that's taken care of, whip up some rice. I prefer brown rice cos it tastes a jillion times better than the Anglofied stuff, plus it's healthier for you, but it's up to you, of course, and brown rice does take longer to cook. Anyway, if you're doing up brown rice, put 4 cups of water and 2 cups of rice (rice is almost always cooked in a 2:1 ratio to water) in a pan. Bring it to a boil, and when it starts boiling, turn the heat down and let it simmer for 45 minutes or so until it's nice and fluffy and ricey.

While you're cookin' up the rice, chop up a buncha vegetables. I don't care what kind you put in--it's up to you and your taste buds--but I recommend ones like bok choy, bean sprouts, chives, tomatoes, corn (off the cob--fuck cans), mushrooms, snow peas and the pod, onions, water chestnuts, zucchini, and if I'm feeling a little crazy I throw in a couple diced up bell peppers or maybe some

broccoli. Chop 'em up to whatever size will fit in your mouth. Be creative, cut out little stars or circle @'s or somethin'.

Anyway, when the rice is about 30 minutes into the simmer (if you're cooking brown rice; white rice cooks in 20 minutes or so), put a couple tablesppons or so of oil in your wok (or large frying pan, as the case may be), heat it up, and dump in some diced hard tofu. At this time you want to add the first wave of spices. Like the vegetables, my choice of spices varies, but they usually include the three C's (curry powder, coriander, cumin), pepper, ginger, garlic powder and/or garlic salt, and of course lemon pepper.
These aren't all specifically "Chinese" spices, but who cares? They taste good. Dump a healthy dose of each plus your own in the tofu, and fry it up for about 5-7 minutes, or until it tastes cooked.

Next add your veggies, except the tomatoes, which you'll want to add last so they'll be just heated yet still crisp when you eat them, which provides for good texture and color and of course flavor. Dump 'em in on top of the tofu and add the second wave of spices. Mix 'em all around and cook till the veggies start to soften.

At this point you'll want to add a sauce to wet things up a bit. There's a bunch of ways to do this. One is to mix 1 1/2-2 tablespoons or so of corn starch in one cup of warm water and a teaspoon of soy sauce. Pour over the mixture and let cook for five minutes or so--it creates a nice sauce. You can also use black bean sauce, or even cheat and buy stir-fry seasonings and just dump the bottle or packet in the wok (check the ingredients before you buy!). Whatever, but cook the stir-fry for five minutes or so or until the veggies are cooked yet still a bit crunchy, and then toss in the tomato wedges and stir and cook for a minute.

By this time your rice should be done, so get out a plate, plop some rice on it (I like to top it with a chunk of soy margarine), and then spoon out some scrumptious stir-fry on top. Jack likes to top it all off with chow mein noodles and a dash of soy sauce--so do I. This is a great summer dish, but it's good 365 days of the year (but not 365 days in a row). Yeah! Wok on! Long live Wok! Wok 'n roll high school! For those about to Wok, we salute you!

Jack's "Bring Back Black Sabbath Bean Casserole"

I made this once for the B.S. crew on their 76 tour and tried to bring it back stage but they wouldn't let me in (not cute enough I guess). Wayne ate the remains.

One onion
One green pepper
5-10 moshrooms
one block tofu (optional)
one tomato
16 oz. can tomato sauce
3 cans chili beans (or equivalent)
1/2 cup\nutritional yeast
several flour tortillas (no LARD!)
1 tablespoon Cayenne
1 tablespoon Chili Powder
1 tablespoon Cumin
stale tortilla chips (optional)
Eryc S&*^%$#$% (optional but pertinent for leftovers)

Sautee' onions and moshrooms and green pepper until tender. Add tomatoes and sauce- let simmer for about 20 minutes. Add beans (drain out sauce in cans), add yeast and spices. Stir another 10 minutes. Preheat oven to 350 and align casserole dish with tortillas. Add layers of mixture and put tortillas in to separate layers. Throw in stale chips wherever possible. Bake for 20-30 minutes or until top tortilla is brown. This aint heaven it's cornucopia!

Jack's Tantalizing Tamale Pie

Not sure why this is called "Tamale" pie, since their are no tamales in it. We are rebels, so there! This is sure to be a double D-O-S-S.

2 cups corn bran
3 cups water
1 can corn (16 oz.) (or equivalent)
1 can tomato sauce (8 oz.)
2 tablespoons oil
1 onion (diced)
2 green peppers
2 cans chili beans (16 oz.)
2 tablespoons cayenne pepper
2 tablespoons chili powder
2 tablespoons black pepper
1/4 lb. nutritional yeast

Pour corn bran into boiling water, slowly, until it makes a nice, clumpy mass. As soon as bran is added turn oven to LOW. Mix it around a bit. Spread mixture around casserole dish, covering sides and bottom. Fry onion and add peppers until soft. Add beans and tomatoes, simmer for 10 minutes, add spices and yeast. Pour mixture into casserole dish and bake at 325 for 25 minutes. Enjoy! Best served with chips and listening to HOPEFUL MONSTERS! HA!

Rosti-Pie   by Kristel De Geest

Grate 4-5 potatoes. Stir in some soy sauce and nutritional yeast flakes. Put this in a greased pie dish and bake for 45 minutes in a 350 degree oven.

Meanwhile, make the filling. Slice one cauliflower in little flowers. Sauté them in some water. Add some cubed smoked tempeh toghether with herbs (whatever you prefer).

After a few minutes, add three sliced tomatoes. After 5-10 minutes, stir in some tomato paste. Put this mix on the rosti-pie shell bottom after it has cooked. Strew some sesame seed and yeast flakes on top, and put it all back in the oven and bake for 20 minutes. Serve with a green salad.

Lentil and Mushroom Bake   by Christy Colcord

This stuff rules. Even my diehard carnivore friends like it and make it themselves now and then. I like it hot, but freak on it cold, too, as a spread/paté.

8 oz red lentils (washed)
1 large onion, chopped
2 cloves garlic, minced
a whole bunch of mushrooms, chopped/sliced
margarine
thyme
coriander
oregano
basil
black pepper
1 teaspoon yeast extract (or miso)
1 tablespoon (or more) of tomato pureé (paste will also do)
1 vegetable stock cube (or other veggie stock extract)
4 oz wholemeal breadcrumbs (1/2 cup), less if using as a paté

Preheat oven at 375 degrees (190C). Grease a 2 pint (1 liter) ovenproof dish or regular-size breadpan.

Put lentils and stock cube in a pan, bring to a boil in water, and skim off any froth. Cover and simmer on low heat for 20 minutes, until lentils are soft and mushy. Drain off water.

Melt margarine and sauté onions, garlic, and mushroms until soft. Add to lentils, then add seasonings, yeast extract, and tomato pureé. Mix up thoroughly and add half the breadcrumbs.

Pile all the mixture into the dish and smooth over the top. If serving hot, add breadcrumbs to top. If cold, sprinkle just a few, not the whole load. Bake for 30 minutes. Great on toast cold with margarine! Can be frozen, cooked or uncooked.

Why
by Tom Scut

I'm a vegan because I choose not to contribute to the pain and misery of this planet. It horrifies me that people kill other beings and consume their bodies. It horrifies me more that I was once as blind and ignorant and brainwashed as to believe that death was food. As for dairy products, I find using the milk of other species very unnatural. I wonder how people would react to human milk products (yogurt, cheese, etc.). Pretty gross, yet they consume cow's milk. Dairy is a very sexist thing as well; it's female cows being raped, milked, and having their offspring ripped from them. As for leather and such I wear my own skin, it's enough I think. I guess I sound angry, but it hurts so much to see other beings murdered, tortured and exploited for the greed and gluttony of human beings. I think veganism could change the world and the beings on it, so I do as I believe. . .

Lentils and Eggplant   **by Tom Scut**

Sauté: *1 onion, chopped*
            4 cloves garlic, chopped
            In a small amount of oil in a big pot.
Add: *1 large eggplant, peeled and cubed*
     Cook for a few minutes until eggplant and onions and garlic are browning a bit.
Add: *1 1/2 cups washed and drained lentils*
            Stir around.
Add: *3 cups water*
            1 large can tomato sauce, or two tomatoes, chopped small
Add: *1 teaspoon salt*
            2 teaspoons sweetener (succanat, rice syrup, etc.)
            1/2 teaspoon cayenne pepper
            1 teaspoon cumin and/or coriander, ground
            You can change the spices to suit your taste.
     Cook until lentils are soft, about 40 minutes on low flame.
     Tastes great on top of pasta.

The Best Goddamn Fried Potatoes You've Ever Eaten   by joel
Cookin' Tunes: Last Option "Burning" (It's a great LP plus Jeff
is a total potatohead)
"Exclusion" compilation LP

This is a fucking great thing to cook, it's so goddamned delicious. It's best eaten after you win a tough hockey game 7-4 in the playoffs against the best team in the league and you're a bit buzzed cos you drank too much post-game beer and you have the total munchies, but, uh, I make it for dinner a lot, too.

potatoes, 9-12
onions, 1-2
green onions (scallions), 1-2 bunches
tofu, 1 pound

corn on the cob, 1-2 cobs
kidney beans, 1 can or 1 cup cooked yourself
green bell peppers, 2-4
mushrooms, handful or two
zucchini, 1 if you feel like it
tomatoes, 2-3
spices: garlic powder, garlic salt, lemon pepper, cayenne pepper,
*   cumin, coriander, curry powder, ground basil leaves, black*
*   pepper, chili pepper, etc.*
any other veggies you may fancy (like chile peppers)

Take the potatoes, wash them well, and dice the fuckers up. The smaller you dice 'em the faster they cook; do 'em about thumbnail size. You just do that, then put a good bit of oil in a wok or BIG frying pan. Heat the oil, then put the potatoes in. Put in a healthy dose of all the spices and cook for 10-15 minutes, until the potatoes are 2/3 cooked (guess at this). Stir constantly so the potatoes don't burn. Quick, you're losing your buzz, so grab a homebrew. Whew, okay. While this stuff is frying, chop up the onions, scallions, mushrooms, bell peppers, zucchini, corn, and chiles (if you got 'em).

Grab another beer. Like I said, when the potatoes are 1/2-2/3 cooked (kinda soft but still crunchy on the inside), sloppily dice up a 1 pound block of tofu and dump it in the wok with the potatoes and spices. Be amazed at the loud popping noises as water meets burning oil. You may need to add more oil once while cooking, as potatoes soak up a lot. Okay, fry this up until the tofu is mostly done (ditto for the potatoes) and dump in your diced veggies and the can of kidney beans. Add a fuckload more spices at this point, too. Keep stirring constantly. Cook 'til it's edible to you, tossing in some tomato wedges at the very last second (this keeps them crunchy and adds a lot to the texture).

Turn the stove off and dallop yourself up a huge portion (I like to place a huge chunk of vegan margarine on top and sometimes a little soy sauce, when I'm feeling a little crazy) with another beer and some saltines and pig out. Now, you're tipsy, you're full, you're tired, the record's over, and you're stoked. Go to bed, and save the rest for lunch tomorrow.

Barley and Pea Casserole   by Kris Curtis

1 onion, chopped
1 cup yellow split peas
2 1/2 cups water
1/2 cup pearl barley
2 tablespoons chopped parsley
1 teaspoon dill seed
1/4 cup sliced mushrooms

Sauté onions until tender, add peas, and cook 5 minutes. Add 1/2 cup water and barley and cook for 2 minutes. Add remaining water, parsley and dill and reduce heat and simmer for 55 minutes, until the liquid is absorbed. Add mushrooms and cook 5 minutes.

Black-Eyed Bean Cutlets by Anita Harris and Paul Wain

1 1/4 cups black-eyed beans, soaked overnight
8 chopped spring onions
2 grated carrots
2 crushed garlic cloves
1 tablespoon soy sauce
2 teaspoons curry powder
2 tablespoons chopped coriander
salt and pepper
1 cup bread crumbs

Drain beans, place in pan and cover with cold water. Bring to boil. Boil rapidly 10 minutes, then cover and simmer 20-25 minutes until tender. When tender, drain well, then mash.

Add all remaining ingredients except for breadcrumbs. Mix well. Shape into 8 ovals and flatten to 1 cm thick. Mix some curry powder with breadcrumbs and use to coat cutlets completely.

Fry in hot, shallow oil for 4 minutes on each side. Serves 4.

Ratatouille by Mike Juhre

1 onion, peeled and chopped
1 small eggplant, diced into 1 inch cubes
2 small bell peppers, quartered and sliced
3 medium zucchini, cut into 1/4" slices
1 small cucumber, peeled, seeded, and diced
2-3 cloves garlic, pressed or minced
1 small hot red pepper, finely minced
4 tablespoons olive oil
2 cups vegetable broth
3/4 cup tomato paste
3 tomatoes, cut in eighths
vinaigrette dressing (blend 1/4 cup vinegar, 1 tablespoon lemon
*   juice, 1 teaspoon dijon mustard or 1/4 teaspoon dry mustard,*
*   1/2 cup olive oil, salt and pepper*

Heat olive oil in large skillet. Add red pepper and garlic. Saute 2-3 minutes, add onion. Saute 3-4 minutes, then add zucchini, eggplant, and bell peppers. Toss so oil evenly coats vegetables (within reason--don't have a cow if it ain't perfect). In a bowl, mix broth and tomato paste, then add to skillet. Add cucumbers. Cook slowly (on low or medium low heat) for about an hour or until liquid is absorbed. Vegetables should be tender but not mush. Just before taking the skillet off the heat, add the tomatoes and stir.

Serve hot with rolls/bread or cold tossed in vinaigrette. Serves six to eight.

Lentils and Tomatoes   by Kris Curtis

1 medium onion, chopped
1 clove garlic, minced
1 1/2 cup dried lentils
4 cups water
1/2 teaspoon black pepper
1/4 teaspoon basil
1/4 teaspoon oregano
1 cup chopped mushrooms
2 cups stewed tomatoes
1 6 oz can of tomato paste
1 tablespoon vinegar

Saute onions and garlic until the onions are transparent. Add the remaining ingredients and bring to a boil. Turn down heat and simmer uncovered for about 1 hour or until lentils are tender, stirring occasionally. May be served plain or over brown rice or whole wheat noodles.

JAY AND MISSYS SPICY STUFFED PEPPERS

1 block tofu
1 large onion
2 tbs olive oil
2 tbs soy sauce
1 cup water
6 oz. tomato paste
1 tsp. chili powder
1 tbs. vinegar
1 tsp. sea salt
2 tbs. nutritional yeast
2 tsp. dry mustard
1/2 tsp garlic
1/2 tsp. black pepper
2 tbs. brown sugar
3 large green peppers

Freeze tofu then thaw by placing in a pot of boiling water. Slice onion and then fry in oil until soft. Tear tofu into small pieces then add to onion. Fry together for a few minutes adding more oil if needed. Stir in soy sauce, ad tomatoe paste and water, mix thoroughly. Lower temp. to simmer then mix in chili powder and rest of spices. Cut off tops of peppers, remove seeds and center. Fill center with mixture. Preheat oven to 350F. Place peppers on oiled cookie sheet and bake for 30 or 40 minutes until tender.

Savory Baked Tofu   by Todd/Pollution Circus

Mix (whip) together:
2 tablespoons soysauce/tamari
2 tablespoons peanut butter
1 tablespoon chili powder
1 teaspoon cumin powder

Coat approximately 1 1/2 to 2 pounds of tofu with this mixture, in slices or chunks, however you like. Broil, turning every few minutes. Cook until the tofu puffs up on at least two sides. Use in all types of things: in Indian tacos, nachos, slices on sandwiches, etc.

Tofu Tempura

1 cup flour
1/3 cup corn starch
1 teaspoon arrowroot
1 teaspoon water
oil for frying
tofu

Mix first four ingredients until you get a real sticky goo. Cut tofu into strips about 1/2" thick. Apply batter goo to tofu and deep fry

Brazilian Tofu Vatapa`   by Jackie Weltman

1. Fry tofu in cubes in oil until golden brown. Add chopped onions and tomato and brown.
2. Add:
vegetable stock to fill the pan halfway
1 cup puréed coconut milk and meat or canned cream of coconut
1/2 cup roasted peanuts
1/2 to 1 teaspoon chile powder
1 teaspoon coriander seed, ground
1 teaspoon cumin seed, ground
3. Cook on medium low heat until the sauce has blended and thickened.
Serve with rice.

Spinach Pie   by Lydia Ely

Buy a piecrust without lard in it *(or use the recipe given here ed.).* Bake it for 10 minutes at 400 degrees before you start this.

2 big bunches of fresh spinach--clean and cut off the ends (or 1 box frozen spinach, approx. 10 oz size)
1/3 cup oil or so
2 onions chopped up
1 1/2 pounds tofu
one lemon
salt
nutmeg

Sauté the onion in the oil until it's light brown. Do it slow; they should be soft. Add the spinach and let it cook for a while, until it is wilted (fresh) or thawed (frozen). Crumble the tofu and add it in. Put on juice from 1/2 lemon and about 3 pinches of salt and a quick dash of nutmeg. Put it all in the pie shell and bake 30-40 minutes at about 400 degrees.

Warning: Before you put it all in the shell, try to drain off the extra liquid.

Spinach Veggie Rolls   by Todd/Pollution Circus

First, make a pastry dough:
3 cups unbleached flour
3/4 cup margarine
cold water

Blend flour and margarine. Add just enough cold water to form a soft dough. Make wrappers by separating pastry dough into ten balls and roll out into squares between 1/4 and 1/2 inch thick.

For the stuffing:
2 or 3 bunches spinach
3 teaspoons vegetable oil
1/4 cup chopped onions
1/4 cup chopped bell pepper
1 tablespoon oregano
6 oz tomato paste
1/2 teaspoon paprika
1/2 teaspoon garlic powder
1 cup cooked rice
1 pound crumbled tofu

Steam spinach until cooked, drain and place in a large mixing bowl. Add the rest of the ingredients and then spoon out the mixture onto the pastry dough "wrappers". Roll or fold and bake at 350 degrees for about 15 minutes.

Pink Cauliflower by Kristel De Geest

1 cauliflower
250g (approx. 1 1/4 cups) mushrooms
nutritional yeast flakes
225g (approx. 8 oz.) tofu
tomato paste
soy milk
1 lemon
mustard
breadcrumbs
ground almonds
sesame seeds
margarine

Mix the last four ingredients. Put this in a greased ovenproof dish. In the meanwhile, sauté the sliced cauliflower together with the mushrooms. Stir in some yeast flakes.

Put the breadcrumb mixture in the oven for 15 minutes at 400 degrees.

Mash the tofu. Stir in juice of the lemon and the tomato paste. Add soymilk and add mustard to taste.

Put the vegetables on the breadcrumb mixture after it's baked, then put the tofu on top. Put in the oven again for approximately 20 minutes.

Fried Cauliflower   by Kamala

This is a very simple recipe, but it does take a certain amount of finesse to have it not come out like mush. This is a Lebanese dish and, as with all Arab food, it must be eaten with lavash or pita bread. If you dare to use a fork to eat it, and ancient Lebanese curse will be put upon you, so be proper and use your hands to eat this!

1 head of cauliflower
olive oil
salt
pepper
lavash or pita bread
soy butter

Cut up the cauliflower into medium-sized flowerettes. In a medium frying pan, pour enough olive oil in to cover the bottom of the pan thoroughly. Preheast pan over a medium-high heat. Carefully throw the cauliflower in and salt and pepper. Fry cauliflower for about 7 minutes, stirring only once during that time (if you stir the cauliflower too much, it turns to mush). Reduce heat to low-medium and cover for about ten minutes. Pierce a fork through to test for tenderness. It should be relatively tender. Take cover off and turn heat back up to medium-high. Salt and pepper and fry until the cauliflower is very brown or burnt (it tastes really good burnt). Again, stir only once to get the cauliflower browned evenly. Eat with plenty of bread and butter. Serves one if you're a pig like me or four if you're a normal person.

Editor's note: We've tried this recipe several times here at the HippyHouse, and we can only give it the highest of recommendations. We add a healthy dose of curry powder when we make it, too. Yum!

Vegan Moshed Potatoes   by joel
Tunes: anything with a good mosh beat

Yo, me an' da bros like to eat dis before a big YOT/Gorilla Biscuits gig at CB's, ya know?

Lots of potatoes (8-9 medium-sized or so)
soy milk
margarine
nutritional yeast
lemon pepper
pepper

Clean and dice up a bunch of potatoes in about 1 inch cubes (no need to be picky). Fill up a big pot about half to 2/3 full of potatoes, then fill up the rest with water and boil.

When the potatoes are soft enough to stick a knife easily through them (about 15-20 minutes), take them off da stove and strain the water. Add about a half stick of margarine and 1/4 cup of soy milk and a healty dash of yeast flakes and lemon pepper and stir. If you have a mixer, use that, but whatever you do, be sure you mosh them in a counterclockwise direction!

If the potatoes are still dry, slowly add margarine and soy milk until you reach the desired moshed potato consistency. Be sure not to add too much soy milk or margarine, cos while it's easy to add more liquid to dry potaotoes, if you make your potatoes too soupy you're fucked.

Mix in more lemon pepper and black pepper as desired, and then scarf. Be sure not to spill any on your $90 leather Nikes.

My Ex-Wife's Stuffed Cabbage   by Jackie Weltman

1. Remove core from 1 large head of green cabbage and steam for 5 minutes to soften leaves.
2. Filling: Saute 1 diced onion until soft. Stir in 1 cup raw brown rice and saute a few minutes. Add 1 1/2 cup veggie stock, 2 tablespoons raisins, 1/4 cup slivered almonds, chopped celery, 1/2 teaspoon cinamon, 1/2 teaspoon salt, and a dash of black pepper. Simmer for 30 minutes.
3. When rice is cooked, wrap 1 tablespoon of filling in each cabbage leaf, tuck in and roll up.
4. Place rolls seam side down in a lightly oiled baking dish. Spread with sauce (see step 5) and bake 45 minutes at 350 degrees.
5. To make the sauce, saute 1 onion in oil. Stir in 1 teablespoon flour and cook 2-3 minutes. Add 2 cups fresh or canned chopped tomatoes, 1 cup tomato juice or sauce, dash pepper, 1/2 teaspoon salt, and 1/4 teapsoon cloves (optional).

Metaphysical Macaroni Casserole (j@)

In order to cook this scrumpcious dish you must first look deep within yourself and answer some fundamental questions. "Do I exist?", "If I did, would I eat?", "Is that oven actually hot? Or merely a cognitive schema invented by humans that holds no value in the real world?" To answer all these questions, turn the knob on your oven to HI. Wait 5 minutes. Place your hand on the oven. The scream of agony could only come from one hungry and hurting individual.

24 oz. pasta (mac noodles)
water for boiling
6 tablespoons vegetable shortening
6 tablespoons whole wheat flour
4 cups soy (not oi) milk
1 block tofu
1 tablesppon garlic salt
1 tablespoon black pepper
1/3 lb. nutritional yeast
one lb. moshrooms
1 1/2 onions

Put pasta in water, let boil about 20 minutes while you cut up veggies. Cut up onions, moshrooms, tofu (1" blocks), set aside. Melt margarine in saucepan add flour and soy (not oi) milk until it boils. Add yeast until it thickens like lava. Let simmer for 10 minutes. Drain macaroni and put it into casserole dish with veggies. Slowly pour sauce over mixture being careful to even it out (mix well dummy!). Bake this for 30 minutes at 350. Serve with a nice boiled vegetable (broccoli is great) and hot bread sticks.

Tofu Chile Rellanos   by Jotham

tortillas
whole green chiles (canned or fresh roasted, 1 per serving)
tofu (1 block)
nutritional yeast (1 cup, or to taste)
cayenne pepper
black pepper
diced onions
diced garlic

Mix tofu, yeast, spices and onion. Stuff mixture into green chiles. Wrap in tortillas and deep fry in oil.

WHY VEGAN?

We have both been vegan well over a year now and have not looked back since. While vegetarianism is obviously an important step for animal liberation (one of many reasons to change your diet) veganism is often looked over as "too extreme" "too difficult" or even "unnecessary".

We both stopped eating meat when we got involved in animal rights. However, to be concerned about the murder of non human animals as well as the treatment of animals for medical and cosmetic reasons yet ignore the tortures of the dairy and egg industry seems quite hypocritical.

First of all milks soul purpose is to feed calves not humans. Because of human greed milk is taken for human consumption and the calves are taken away from their mothers. Then the calves spend their short life as part of the veal trade. Buying and using dairy products directly supports perhaps the ugliest form of agribusiness, veal. Dairy cows do not live a happy peaceful existence either. Factory farming is factory farming and this means animals are treated like machines with no concerns or feelings. dairy cows are kept in dirty, cramped, concrete stalls which they never leave. They are milked only once a day as opposed to twenty times a day by their calves naturally- causing extreme discomfort and deformed udders. Then after the dairy cow has been raped and abused by humans a few years and her body has worn out and she cannot supply milk she is slaughtered after all she is now of no use to the money hungry business people.

The egg industry is another disgusting example of animal mistreatment. Chickens are crowded in tiny pens. They are debeaked so they will not fight under their abnormal conditions. Then they are fed anti biotics so they can lay ridiculous amounts of eggs no matter what their health is like.

Animal products sneak into your food if you're not careful. Rennet, which comes from the lining of calves stomachs is used to coagulate cheese. In our opinions cheese shouldn't even be considered a vegetarian food! There are also things like gelatin and lard which are direct byproducts of the slaughterhouse. Honey is another thing to avoid. It's totally unnecessary and easy to without. Animal exploitation should not be considered less if a bee or a cow.

Another thing we've come to eliminate from our diet is artificial additives. Most of these products are human made chemicals and no doubt tested on animals. Personally we prefer to eat food, not chemicals. They don't seem to be particularly healthy either, ingesting substances whose names cannot even be pronounced is not particularly enticing.

We feel that becoming a complete vegan is one of the most important and crucial steps that should be taken by those of us who dream of animal liberation. However veganism is a personal decision.. people should not be cut down for not going vegan, espescially if they are doing other worthwhile things in their lives. (Like boycotting cosmetic companies that test). We both encourage people to adopt "cruelty free" lifestyles but we don't choose friends

and reject others because of their views on the subject. People like Sean of VEGAN REICH can fuck off with their nazi attitudes. People need to be educated not dictated to.

Well if we didn't mention the environmental reasons for going vegan I suppose we will leave that to someone else. Special thanx to the HIPPYCORE folx for doing this extremely worthwhile project and letting people like us voice our opinions on this important subject. Cook up a storm!

Jason and Missy Bushwacker
Po Box 23
S. Gardiner Me. o4359

RAKESH THE CHEF CHOLLA MASSALA
(Garbanzo beans in Indian Curry)

Onion
Ginger root
Garlic
Tomatoes
oil for frying
chili powder
tumeric powder
flannel seeds powder
garam massala (check Indian store)
garbanzo beans

Grind onions, ginger root and a few pieces of garlic. Grind tomatoes and keep them separate. Heat oil in a pan and put paste onions, ginger, and garlic in until it is thick and dark brown in color Put Garbanzo beans in paste above (add a little water too). After

paste has stuck firmly to the beans put in water and pressure cook for 3-4 minutes. Serve with rice.

Mesquite Smoked Tempeh with Rich Mole Sauce--"Mole Poblando"
by Jackie Weltman the Goddess

"Totally amazing," this is one of my absolute favorites.

1. To Grill Tempeh: a) Marinate tempeh overnight in garlic, chile, soy and lime juice. b) soak mesquite chips in water for several hours. Drain and place on hot coals. c) Cover grill with tempeh, drained. Add soaked chips as necessary to generate smoke. Cook until you're satisified. If you want, baste the tempeh with the sauce.

2. To Make the Sauce: a) saute

> *1 large onion*
> *5 cloves garlic*
> *1 teaspoon ground star anise*
> *1/2 teaspoon ground cloves*
> *1 teaspoon cinnamon*
> *1 teaspoon ground coriander*
> *1 teaspoon ground sesame seeds*
> *1 ground stale tortilla*

b) Add three diced tomatoes to the saute. Simmer on low. c) Deseed 5 ancho or mulato chiles (dried, red chiles). Toast lightly in skillet, the just cover with hot veggie broth or water. Let soak 20 minutes. Place in blender and puree. Add to saute. d) Beat in 1 can tomato paste and 1 tablespoon sugar. Simmer ten minutes. e) Place 2 oz unsweetened dark chocolate (or Mexican chocolate if you can find it) in skillet and melt into sauce. Simmer 15 more minutes. Add more chile if you want it more spicy. Serve over tempeh. Yippee!

Curry--cheap and exotic and easy and great   **by Lydia Ely**

The key here is the spices; the veggies you choose don't really matter. Another key is lots of margarine. You'll need a big saucepan/kettle with a lid.

margarine--lots, not oil
onions
spices: curry powder, turmeric, cumin, coriander, cardoniom, cloves,
*   cinnamon (lots of "c" words), cayenne, salt*
vegetables: choose from zucchini, mushrooms, cauliflower, potatoes,
*   chick peas, eggplant, carrots, spinach, etc.*
add nuts if you are rich: cashews, etc.
tofu, if you like (cube and fry in oil first)
condiments: raisins, bananas (smushed), chutneys ($pricey$),
*   shredded coconut, cucumber, etc.*

Cook chopped onions in lotsa margarine for a while, until they are transparent. Add <u>lots</u> of spices now (if you add them later, they'll have no effect). Decide how hot you want it to be with the cayenne. Curry powder and cumin should be the main ones--the others help. Salt freely. Cook for a while til the margarine seems to dry up, then start adding vegetables and some water or vegetable stock pronto. Vegetables should be roughly the same size as each other. Use tons of vegetables or just 1 or 2 kinds, but make sure you have adequate liquid to cover vegetables. Cover and turn heat down. Cook 1 hour or so.

If you're using potatoes, smash some down at the end--they'll make a kind of gravy. If you have too much liquid and it isn't "stewy" enough, take off lid and cook at higher heat for a while and the water will evaporate.

At the end add nuts. Serve with cute little dishes of condiments and your guests will be impressed. Serve with rice or rice pilaf, or rice with saffron and peas (nice). Yum.

SWEET AND SOUR TOFU ALA' J@CKCHAN

This is not a favorite at the HC pad cuz' Joel is too wimpy too appreciate sweet and sour and Audrey is just plain scared. Anyway I make it whenever I get a date (rarely I realize). It should satisfy your alternate egos with the sweet and sour combo.

1 cup sugar
2 tablespoons cornstarch
1 teaspoon salt
1 teaspoon cinnamon
2 tablespoons ginger
1/4 cup lemon juice
1/2 cup white wine vinegar
1/4 cup soy (obviously not oi) sauce
2 blocks tofu (16 oz.)
veggies of your choice (peas and carrots are nice)
1 can pineapple chunks. (Reserve juice for sauce below)

Combine first 8 ingredients and pineapple juice in a saucepan and heat. Cut tofu into 1/2" blocks and stirfry over medium heat.in a separate pan. When sauce thickens add it to tofu and vegetables as well. Lastly add the pineapple chunks and you are set.

Indira's Favorite Curry

When I was heavily into Gandhi, non violence etc... I met Indira at a SLOPOKE gig in D.C. She gave me this recipe and told me it would help in the struggle.

1 onion
1 head cauliflower
5 potatoes
8 cups water
curry (to taste)
cumin "
ginger "
coriander "
2 tablespoons Peanut Butter

Sautee onion (diced) with spices in a saucepan until tender. Add water, potatoes, cauliflower, and boil about 30 minutes, adding spices all the way. Your last step would be to add P. Butter.

Baba Ghanouj (Sesame Eggplant Spread)   by Mike Juhre

1 pound eggplant
1/4 cup taratour sauce (see recipe below)
1/4 cup fresh lemon juice
1 teaspoon salt
1/4 teaspoon pepper
1 tablespoon + 1 teaspoon olive oil
2 tablespoons fresh cilantro, chopped

Prick eggplant with fork in several places and roast in 400 degree oven for 45-55 minutes or until soft throughout. Let eggplant cool, then cut in half and scrape out the pulp. Mince pulp and add it to taratour sauce, lemon juice, salt and pepper, and 1 tablespoon olive oil. Mix thoroughly and correct seasonings to taste. Spread in shallow dish, drizzle remaining 1 teaspoon olive oil on top, and sprinkle with cilantro. Chill well before serving. Serve with crackers or hot pita bread.

Channa Pindi   by Donna Rivest
An Indian dish

1 cup cooked chick peas (garbanzo beans)
2 tablespoons oil
2 cloves garlic, minced
2 teaspoons ginger, minced
2 cups cook Basmati rice

Saute garlic in oil and add ginger and chickpeas. Saute for a few minutes so chickpeas are heated through. Serve over hot rice.

Bahmie Goreng With Nuts (Fried Noodles)
by Anita Harris and Paul Wain

1/2 pound wheat or soy noodles
4 cups water
1 cup coarsely chopped nuts (peanuts, almonds, or cashews)
3 tablespoons oil
1/2 teaspoon coriander
1/2 teaspoon caraway seed
dried chili to taste
1-2 cloves garlic, minced
1-2 slices fresh ginger root, minced
2-3 onions, chopped
1/4-1/2 cabbage, shredded
1-2 cups of other shredded vegetables (carrotss, yams, parsnip,
    capsicum, leek)
4 tablespoons soy sauce
1 tablespoon honey
1 tablespoon hot water

Cook noodles in 4 cups water until tender (5-10 minutes). Set aside for use later.

Cook nuts in oil until lightly browned (3-5 minutes). Remove nuts from oil and drain for use later. Increase heat and add onions, garlic, ginger, and spices and fry in the oil until onions are soft.

Add cabbage and chopped vegetables to onions and cook until just soft, then add noodles and fry for 2-3 minutes.

Combine soy sauce, honey, and hot water and mix until honey dissolves, then add to noodles and vegetables. Simmer for 3-4 minutes so noodles can absorb liquid. Add nuts when about to serve.

We will never have peace until we have reached a stage of true anarchy. Anarchy is love. Love is the respect for another that can only make this world a better place. Love, respect and mutual understanding of all creatures can only make us the true keepers of this planet. When bound by love and respect for each other, then and only then will peace be accomplished and there will be an end to all senseless killing and hatred on planet earth. --Troll

Pasta Sauce   by Troll

2 35 oz (875 grams) cans "stewed" or "peeled" tomatoes "in water"
1 8 oz can tomato paste
4-10 leaves fresh basil (coarsely chopped)
8 oz fresh garden mushrooms (chopped)
1 medium green bell pepper (chopped)
2 teaspoons oregano (or substitute with fresh oregano, if possible)
1/2 teaspoon black pepper
2-3 cloves fresh garlic, finely chopped

Combine everything in a large pot and bring to a boil, then simmer for 30 minutes. You may wish to cut the tomatoes before heating but they will break up during cooking to a degree. Remember to stir continuously to avoid burning!

Some options to think about: Use 8-10 fresh medium tomatoes (chopped into 1 inch pieces) if they are cheaply available. Some additional vegetables you may want to add could be red or yellow bell peppers, yellow squash, zucchini, broccoli, etc.

Serve on rotini noodles (spirals), preferably of the vegetable or "rainbow" variety. Also goes on spinach fetucini noodles.

TOFU LASAGNA J@CK (Lord Of Aggression) STYLE

First of all the sauce and Tofu mixture here can be used in several other Italian dishes (Ravioli, Canoli, stuffed shells etc..) so please apply where applicable. This takes a while to prepare so make sure it's for a special occasion (a revolution, Eryc fasts, Walt stops buying records etc...)

J@ck "The Italian Stallion" FAMOUS SAUCE

one onion
3 cloves garlic
10 8 oz. cans tomatoe sauce (not generic brand)
1 tablespoon sugar
3 tablespoons garlic salt (To Taste)
3   basil leaves
3   oregano
3   black pepper
2   bay leaves (not south bay)

Saute' sliced onion and chopped up garlic until tender and the whole kitchen smells incredible add sauce and spices. Simmer at least two hours on LOW heat. Also you can add Moshrooms, Artichoke hearts, or whatever else fancies you. I like it pretty simple.

5 cups water
16 oz. lasagna noodles
2 blocks tofu
1 cup soy (are you kidding not oi) milk
1/8 lb. nutritional yeast

In Blender blend tofu, soy milk, and yeast. It shouldn't be liquid, just rather chunky. Put this aside. Boil pasta noodles around 15 minutes or so until soft. If they are too long to fit into your pot then don't be afraid to break em' in 1/2! When cooked align the bottom of a long casserole pan with noodles. Cover with sauce, tofu mix, and sprinkle nutritional yeast. Repeat until dish is completely filled. Bake at 375F for about 30 minutes. This is sure to please you once, or twice.

VEGAN PIZZA J@CKARONI STYLE

This is another one of those dishes you don't want to make unless you have a lot of time. It's something that will please even the biggest bitcher (hi Mondo).

THE DOUGH:

4 cups flour
1 package dry yeast
1 1/4 cup water
3 tablespoons margarine

Combine flour and yeast. Heat water and margarine. Add to dry stuff and beat. Kneed about 10 minutes or so. Place in a greased bowl covered about 50 minutes to rise.

THE SAUCE

Veggies of your choice

(While dough is rising (as well as the AMEBIX) make this)

Please refer to my pasta sauce except double the bay leaves and Basil. While sauce is cooking add veggies of your choice to the sauce (green peppers, onions, whatever you like)

FINALLY

Tofu
Nutritional Yeast

Punch dough down. Roll into two 12" circles (but squares work too- we aren't CIRCLIST). Sprinkle nutritional yeast on the dough. Spread each with the sauce mixture. Now add tofu in chunks on the top and add a load more nutritional yeast. Bake at 400F for 30-35 minutes and whallah! BARROS is bummed!

VEGANISM: A STEP BEYOND VEGETARIANISM by Tammy TTU

My choice to become vegetarian stemmed from a moral objection to the murder of animals strictly to satisfy man's greedy and barbaric lust for animal flesh along with their quest for the almighty dollar- for monetary gain animals are being slaughtered and kept in inhumane conditions and consequently people were starving so I could have my meat and the greedy bastards profited all along. That is what prompted me to become a vegetarian.

My choice to become vegan was due to yet another moral objection. An objection to the view people had of animals. Animals are viewed as tools, milk and meat machines, unfeeling creatures. I felt an objection to the condition in which dairy ,cows were kept, an objection to the space battery hens were given to lay eggs. An objection to people's incessant need to rely on animals for things we could supply ourselves with: protein, calcium, etc.. all the while sparing cruelty to animals while meeting our dietary needs (free of the anti-biotics, toxins, steroids, found in meat and dairy products). In my choice of veganism animals rights weren't the only rights considered, human rights played a role as well.

With only 20% of all food grown in the U.S. being eaten by people, that leaves 80% fed to cattle strictly for profit with total disregard for human health. With one child dying every two seconds meat production seems murderous: calculated, pre meditated murder. If grain, corn, and oats were fed to people instead of cattle starvation could be greatly diminished. 20,000 lbs. of potatoes can be grown on one acre while only 165 lbs. of beef is yielded on the same plot of land.

Veganism is but another branch of vegetarianism, a higher respect for animal and human life, a dedication to living one's life free of all animal exploitation and cruelty that can be avoided. We don't need to exploit animals for our taste buds. There are alternatives all free of animal exploitation.

Low cost, low effort, vegan foods can be made at home. This seeming inconvenience (which lessons in time as you become acquainted with recipes) is well worth it. When you think of all the slaughter, murder, and torture animals endure and realize you aren't a contributor it means a lot.

Tammy- Time To Unite/ Media Children
Po Box 2692
Costa Mesa ca
92626

Carribean Style Yuca or Yam "Curry"   by Jackie Weltman
as made and enjoyed and the Hippycore House

Yuca is a potato-like tuber, slightly sweeter and less starchy than potatoes, that is enjoyed throughout Mexico, Central and South America, the Carribean and Africa. It is available fresh or frozen at Mexican and Central American Markets.

3 large yams or 2 large yuca tubers (yucas peeled of skin)
milk and meat from one small coconut; meat minced or pureed with
*   milk*
1 cup cilantro, fresh leaves only
1 tablespoon chopped garlic
1 small onion, diced
3 very ripe tomatoes, diced
1 red pepper (sweet), diced
1 anaheim chile (the long common green chile pepper at your
*   market), minced*
2 1/2 teaspoons coriander seed
2 teaspoons cayenne pepper
1/2 teaspoon ginger root, ground
1 teaspoon cinnamon

1/2 teaspoon allspice
1/2 teaspoon ground cumin
vegetable oil

1) Heat vegetable oil in wok or large frying pan. Saute garlic, onions and chile until soft over med-high heat. Do not overbrown.
2) Slice yams or yuca thinly and add. Saute until nearly tender.
3) Add spices; mix well.
4) Add tomatoes and cilantro when yams or yuca are completely tender. Saute for five more minutes, then serve.

editor's note: Folks, this dish fucking rules!

Pinto Bean Puree   **by Donna Rivest**
for pinto-wheat bread recipe, below.

1 cup pinto beans (washed, soaked for 8 hours, drained)
2 1/2 cups water
1 tablespoon oil

Bring beans to a boil in the water with oil. Reduce heat and simmer, covered, for 1-1 1/2 hours. Drain, retaining the liquid. Put 2 cups of beans in a blender with 1/2 cup of liquid. Blend on medium.

Pinto-Wheat Bread   by Donna Rivest

Pinto-wheat bread is only one of the <u>few</u> ways I can get my son to willingly eat beans!!

1 cup lukewarm water (90-100 degrees)
1 tablespoon maple syrup
1 package (2 teaspoons) active dry yeast
1 cup pinto bean purée (see recipe above)
2 tablespoons oil
1 teaspoon salt (optional)
2 cups whole wheat flour
3/4-1 1/2 cups unbleached flour

Combine water and syrup in a large bowl. Mix completely, then dissolve yeast in the mixture. Let stand for 15 minutes.

Stir purée, oil, and salt into yeast mixture. Add the whole wheat flour and mix well. Add in enough unbleached flour to make the dough stiff.

Knead on a floured surface for 15 minutes.

Return dough to bowl, lightly oil top of dough and cover with a towel. Let rise in a warm spot (about 75 degrees) until dough has doubled (1 1/2-2 hours).

Punch dough down and then knead 3-4 times. Shape into a loaf. Put dough into an oiled loaf pan.

Cover with towel and let rise again for 45 minutes.

Bake 50 minutes at 350 degrees.

"Build Biscuits Not Bombs"   by joel
Tunes: Final Conflict demo

These are really tasty and the government fears them and their possibilities for creating a just and peaceful world, so take note.

2 cups white unbleached flour
1 tablespoon baking powder
1-2 tablespoons nutritional yeast (optional but delicious)
1 teaspoon salt (optional)
1/3 cup oil
2/3 cup soy milk

Preheat oven to 450 degrees.
Mix all the dry ingredients in a mixing bowl, then add oil and soy milk. Stir until you get a nice soft dough. Eat a little raw; it's good (I think so, anyway). If you're not too lazy, kneading the dough a bit would be a good idea.
Break off little chunks, shape them into little Pentagons, and place them on an ungreased cookie sheet. These really don't rise much, so the size dough ball you put on the cookie sheet will be about the size of the cooked biscuit. Bake until brown on top, about 15-20 minutes.
The sooner you serve them the better, as these taste best hot. If you're cynical about the possibility of these biscuits inducing world disarmament and governmental downfall, let them sit out for a few days and then you can use these biscuits as deadly projectiles to hurl at cops as they drive by your kitchen.
However, I prefer to eat these right out of the oven, topped with margarine and:

Nutritional Yeast Gravy   by joel, adapted/ripped off from *Vegetarian Times Cookbook*

6 tablespoons margarine
1/2 cup nutritional yeast
1/2 cup flour (white unbleached or whole wheat)
3 cups hot water
healthy dash of black pepper
1 clove garlic (optional)

Heat margarine in a medium-sized saucepan. When it's all melted, add the yeast flakes and flour and stir constantly. This creates a *roux*, of which I've written about in another recipe. Cook this doughy concoction for a couple minutes, then slowly and constantly stir in the hot water. You should have a creamy sauce by now. Turn the heat down and add pepper and garlic. Be sure to stir out any clumps of roux (not usually a problem)

<u>Serving Suggestion:</u> A favorite meal of mine is biscuits, this gravy, mashed potatoes (recipe elsewhere), baked tofu (recipe elsewhere), and corn. Hearty, down-home, pseudo-Midwestern and scrumptious! Plus there's lots of nutritional yeast in there to supply you with large amounts of vitamin B12, that vitamin we vegans supposedly can't get from "non-animal sources." Ha! Fuck off, psuedo-health experts!

Joel's Delicious San Francisco Burritos
(dedicated to the Beatnigs and all Bay punx)

This is an easy one, so read up.
Go to San Francisco.
Head to 16th Street between Mission and Valencia. Ask any punk for directions.
Having followed the punk's directions and finding yourself in Oakland, ask someone more reliable for directions and take BART back into the city and back to 16th St.
Walk in to Pacho Villa's Taqueria on 16th between Mission and Valencia, as noted above.
Order a whole bean burrito with rice. Large. Extra spicy (c'mon, don't be scared). If you're feeling really famished, order it with tofu.
Order some fruit juice or Mexican soda in a glass bottle. Don't buy any beverage in plastic if you can avoid it. Plastic sucks.
Pay. It's less than $3, so you're stoked.
Sit down and grub. Best eaten with Martin Sprouse and remember, if you don't have a runny nose and tears streaming down your beet red face after eating this burro, then you really haven't eaten a joel's SF burro.

DESSERTS

J@CK's HIGHLY REQUESTED PEANUT BUTTER CHOCOLATE CHIP COOKIES

I should warn you right away that once you start making these people will never stop bothering you for them. Here is what Joel always does.

A TYPICAL PEANUT BUTTER CHOCOLATE CHIP DIALOGUE
(words in parentheses to be read whispered as if subliminally)

jo: What's up j@ck?

j@: Nothin much.

jo: What are you doing tonight? *(peanutbutterchocolatechipcooookies)*

j@: Probably sit at home, listen to Black Sabbath Volume IV, write some poetry, I dunno why?

jo: I was just wondering *(peanutbutterchocolatechipcookies)*

j@: Why, what are you doing?

jo: I'll probably listen to my Carcass live tape someone recorded on a mini cassette recorder in mono from another building while the concert was going on and do some HC mail *(peanutbutterchocolatechipcookies)*

j@: Maybe I'll make some peanut butter chocolate chip cookies

jo: Good idea.

2 cups Peanut Butter
1/2 cup (one stick) vegan margarine
1 cup sugar
1 cup brown sugar
1 teaspoon vanilla
2 teaspoons arrowroot
2 teaspoons water
3 cups flour
1 1/2 teaspoons baking soda
1 teaspoon salt
splash soy (never even if you are desperate oi) milk
1 package Bakers chocolate chips (12 oz.)

Mix everything in a bowl except chips and soy (never evil oi) milk. Splash soy milk until the texture is somewhere between wet and dry. Add chips. Bake at 350F for 8-10 minutes. This can be smelled from miles away, in fact last time I made these Walt Glazer and Martin Sprouse called simultaneously demanding their share!

Yummy Vegan Chocolate Cookies With Peanut Butter Inside
by Nikole Stepanko

Cookie Dough
1 1/2 cups flour
1/2 cup unsweetened cocoa
1/2 teaspoon baking soda
1/2 cup sugar
1/2 cup firmly packed brown sugar
1/2 cup margarine, softened
1/4 cup peanut butter
1 teaspoon vanilla
1 tablespoon soy lecithin
1 tablespoon water
Filling
3/4 cup peanut butter
3/4 cup confectioners sugar

In a small bowl combine flour, cocoa, and baking soda; blend well. In large bowl, beat sugar, brown sugar, margarine and 1/4 cup peanut butter until light and fluffy. Add vanilla and soy lecithin and water (this is your egg substitute); beat well. Stir in flour mixture until blended and set aside.

In a small bowl, combine filling ingredients; blend well. Roll into 30 one-inch balls. For each cookie, with floured hands shape about 1 tablespoon cookie dough around one peanut butter ball, covering completely. Place 2 inches apart on ungreased cookie sheet. Bake at 375 degrees for 7-9 minutes or until set and slightly cracked. Cool on wire racks. Makes 30.

Anything Cookies   by Max X. Smith

1 cube soy margarine
2 tablespoons brown sugar
3 tablespoons vanilla
dash of salt
2 1/2-3 cups flour
1 20 oz can of pineapple (rings are best)
1-1 1/2 tablespoons baking soda
12 oz dairyless chocolate chips (Baker's semisweet are best)
1 handful raisins
1 handful dried coconut
oats to texture

Preheat oven to 350 degrees, and melt your margarine in the mixing bowl. While you're waiting for that to happen, measure out your flour and baking soda, and mix them. Drain (and save) the juice from the pineapple. Cut the pineapple in small, pizza-shaped pieces.

Blend the margarine, brown sugar, vanilla, and salt. Make sure it's mixed well. Then, alternate adding the flour and pineapple juice, until both are gone.

Mix in the pineapple. Fold in the raisins, coconut, and chocolate chips. Add oats until you get a texture you like. More oats mean drier cookies. Put good-sized scoops on a greased cookie sheet, and bake until done. Yum!

"I'd do **anything** for one of those cookies!"

Banana Shake   by Kristel De Geest

You need a blender for this one.

Break 4 bananas in pieces. Put them in the blender. Add soymilk and apple concentrate. Blend a few minutes.

Variation: add some carob powder.

Lemon Bread   by the Calamity Jane folx

1/2 cup shortening
1 cup sugar
egg substitute equal to 2 eggs (try 2 teaspoons arrow root mixed
*   with 2+ teaspoons water -ed.)*
1 1/4 cup flour
1 teaspoon baking powder
1/2 teaspoon salt
1/2 cup soy milk
1/2 cup nuts (optional)
grated peel of 1 lemon

Mix shortening and sugar until smooth. Add egg substitute, flour, baking powder, salt, soy milk, and grated lemon peel, then pour into greased and floured baking pan. Bake at 350 degrees for about 1 hour; check often.

To make topping, mix 1/4 cup sugar with the juice of one lemon. Pour on top after baking.

Scotch Shortbread   by Jackie Weltman the Master Chef

1 1/4 cup flour
1/4 cup sugar (granulated)
3/4 cup margarine (1 1/2 sticks)
1/2 teaspoon vanilla

Cream margarine and sugar until blended. Add Vanilla. Fold in flour. Mix only until blended. Form into cookies, or to be traditional pat dough into a 9" pie pan. Prick edges with a fork and cut into pie wedged with fork tines. Sprinkle with sugar. Bake at 375 degrees about 20 minutes or until lightly golden. Sprinkle with additional sugar. Pastry will break apart at serrations.

Fruit Cocktail Cake   by Audrey Creed

1 big can syrupy fruit cocktail (use only 1/2 of syrup)
2 cups flour
2 teaspoons baking soda
1/2 teaspoon salt
1 1/2 cups sugar
2 teaspoons arrowroot
2 teaspoons water

1/2 cup brown sugar
1 cup chopped pecans

Mix arrowroot and water for egg substitute. Sift Dry
ingredients together. Add juice from fruit cocktail and arrowroot:
mix. Add the fruit, stir, and then pour in greased pan. Put 1/2 cup
brown sugar and 1 cup chopped pecans over batter. Bake at 350
degrees for about 30 minutes.

Icing for the Cake

3/4 cup sugar
1 stick margarine
1/2 cup soy milk
1 cup shredded coconut

Boil together for 2 minutes, then add coconut. Pour on cake
while still warm. Yum! Very juicy and sweet.

Chocolate Cake   by Todd/Pollution Circus

Here's a foolproof vegan cake recipe that turns out moist, light
and fluffy.

1 1/2 cups unbleached, unenriched white flour
1 cup raw sun evaporated cane juice
3 tablespoons cocoa powder
1 teaspoon baking soda
a generous pinch of salt
1 teaspoon natural vanilla extract
6 tablespoons vegetable oil
generous 3/4 cup of water

Mix dry ingredients, then add liquids. Mix well; it should be a
thick, moist batter. Pour into a lightly oiled 9" square tin. Bake at
350 degrees for 30-35 minutes until a sharp knife inserted comes
out clean.

Raw Apple Cake   **by Audrey   Creed**

2 teaspoons arrow root
2 teaspoons water
1/2 cup oil
2 cups sugar
2 cups flour
pinch of salt
2 teaspoons cinnamon
4 medium size apples, peeled and diced
1 cup chopped walnuts
2 teaspoons baking soda

Mix the arrow root and water; this is your egg substitute. Mix all the ingredients together and bake at 325 degrees for 45-60 minutes.

PEAR SOYA CAKE

6 pieces of pears
SOYA milk 2.5 pints
1 cup soya flour
2 handfulls brown sugar
1/4 teaspoons salt
1 handfull whole grains
9 oz. whole grain flour
1 handful hazlenuts
1 tablespoon margarine
1/4 teaspoon cinnamon

For the production of the dough take a bit of flour and strew it on the table. Put into a bowl the flour and add 1 cup soya milk, salt, and grains. Kneed it for a while. Roll it flat (but not too thin).

Put the remaining soyamilk into another bowl add the sugar and the soya flour, mix it up! Add pear pieces Heat the oven to 300F.

Take   a cake shaped pan, smear the margarine in it, put dough inside. along with the filling. Strew the hazlenuts and cinnamon on top. Put the cake in the oven for about 30-45 minutes. Let it cool down and enjoy!

BY FURZ THE SYSTEM

Baklava   by Jackie Weltman

frozen phyllo dough (usually consists of just flour, water, and starch)
coarsely chopped almonds, walnuts, and/or pistachios to make 2 cups
3/4 cup sugar
1 tablespoon cinnamon
honey syrup

honey syrup
  1 cup honey
  1/3 cup water
  1 teaspoon cinnamon
  1/4 teaspoon nutmeg
  1/4 teaspoon allspice
  1/4 teaspoon grated lemon rind
Combine and simmer on stove.

Mix up nuts, sugar, and the tablespoon of cinnamon. Spread a couple sheets of phyllo on an oven-proof dish. Brush with melted margarine. Sprinkle with nut-sugar mixture. Drizzle honey syrup over. Do it again. And again. Until you've gone as high as you can. Put it in a 350 degree oven to bake and brown. Cool and cut into squares.

Pseudo-Hungarian Pastries   by Todd/Pollution Circus

Well, this is a mockery(?) of something my grandma made for me as a young 'un. I use tofu instead of the flesh; other than it's pretty close to the real thing.

6 cups cabbage, sliced or shredded
1 large onion, sliced
2 pounds tofu-firm, crumbled
2 tablespoons oil
1 tablespoon paprika
1 teaspoon salt
1 teaspoon black pepper
vegan mustard
one vegan pie crust (see recipe elsewhere) divided into four parts

Preheat oven to 400 degrees. Saute the cabbage and tofu and onion in the oil. Add the seasonings while sauteing. Cook until cabbage is done--as tender or firm as you like. Roll out a quarter of the pastry in a rectangular or oval shape, roll to about 1/4 inch thick. Spread a thin layer of mustard on the dough. Place 1/4 of the cabbage tofu mixture down the center of the dough. Fold one side over and roll it over, cut into about 2-3 inch long pieces. Repeat for the other 3 quarters. Place on cookie sheet/baking pan/whatever and bake for 15-25 minutes, until the crust starts to slightly brown.

TOFU BROWNIES (J@)

The first time I made these was at Big Wayne's who loved them but gave them to Chris "the wild one" Wilder for fear of gaining weight. Chris wasn't too worried about it. He already has that kinda sexy physique.

2/3 cup flour
1 1/3 cup water
1 lb. Tofu
1/2 cup soy milk
4 cups sugar
2 teaspoons salt
2 teaspoons vanilla
1 1/2 cup cocoa powder
3 cups flour
2 teaspoons baking powder

In a sauce pan mix together 1 1/3 cup water and 2/3 cup flour. Put tofu in the blender with soy (not oi) milk. Blend them and add to sauce pan. Then add the rest mixing like crazy all the way. Bake in a well oiled and floured pan at 350F about 30 minutes. This will drive you crazy!

Vegan Pie Crust   by Eric "Gretzky" Scudder Butter

This recipe is enough to make both a top and a bottom for one pie. If you need only one crust, halve the recipe. Actually, this recipe is from my Aunt Bernice (Seriously!). She lived on a farm in rural Indiana and cooked for the entire farm crew from before sunrise and until after dark.

1 cup vegetable shortening (Crisco works best)
1/4 cup BOILING water
2 cups flour, unbleached
pinch salt
splash of soy milk (optional--browns the crust)

In a medium sized bowl add the shortening and slowly mix in the hot water until it has a mayonnaise-like consistency (vegan mayo, of course!). You won't use all the water! Add the soy milk and salt. Add flour by cups and stir with a fork.

Take a sponge and wet the counter down. Lay one sheet of wax paper on the damp surface--this anchors the wax paper. Throw some flour on the wax paper and put the dough in the middle. Squash the dough down with your hands and then flour the top of the dough. Throw another sheet of wax paper on top and roll with a rolling pin until the dough is about 1/8" thick.

Now for the tricky part. Take the top sheet of wax paper off carefully and then put the pie pan (upside down) on the dough. With one hand on the pie pan, use the other to scoop underneath and turn over quickly. Peel away the wax paper and take a knife to cut around the perimeter of the pie pan. Flute the edges to make it easier to serve.

Fill the pie shell with whatever goodies you wish. The remaining pie dough should be consolidated for the top crust. You can use any pattern you wish. I cut mine into 3/4" strips and make a lattice arrangement on top.

Note: if you have to cook the shell first, it's okay, too.

Fruit Tarts   **by Todd/Pollution Circus**

O.K., summertime, it's hot out, we're high, got the munchies and fruit is in abundance, and we fruits like tarts at times. They're cool, sweet and feel really good.

First off you'll need a pre-cooked pie crust. Then with your favorite fresh fruit, most any type or a mixture even, fill the pie crust with the fruit cut in whatever way you desire, e.g. whole berries, sliced peaches, etc. For the sauce/glaze retain one cup of fruit and add it to one cup of sweetener (sucunat) in a saucepan and heat on medium low until sugar is liquified and fruit is beginning to cook. Add 2 tablespoons of cornstarch--mix the cornstarch with a small amount (2 tablespoons or so) of water and mix until smooth to avoid clumps of cornstarch. Cook with the cornstarch at least four minutes until it looks clear (when cornstarch is added it will usually

get a bit "milky" looking until is is cooked). Strain this thru a seive/fine colander and if there's still chunks of fruit, mash them through with a spoon. This brings out the natural pectin in the fruit. Scrape the bottom of the seive/colander; this will also remove seeds if need be. Spread over the top of fruit while still a bit warm and liquid. It will soldiidy a bit when fully cool. If you like don't put the sauce on until ready to eat, then heat a little and use it warm.

LOVELY LEMON PIE by J@CK

Let's keep this simple. This is damn good so make it.

3 cups sugar
1/4 cup cornstarch (a bit more actually)
1/2 teaspoon salt
1/2 cup cold water
1/2 cup lemon (or lime) juice
6 teaspoons arrowroot
6 teaspoons water
4 tablespoons margarine
3 cups boiling water
2 (9 inch) pie shells

In a sauce pan combine sugar, cornstarch and salt. Stir in water and lemon juice. Prepare the arrow root and water in a separate cup. Mix them together and add to the rest. Add margarine and boiling water. Heat on MEDIUM until it gets real thick and goopy. Add to the pie shells and refrigerate about 3 hours. Serve. I guess it's a good way to meet girls too if you aren't too shy to deliver them a lemon pie. I am.

Hella Tropical Pineapple Coconut Dessert   by Jackie W.

1 cup shredded coconut
1 pineapple, sliced up
2 cups sugar
3/4 cup pecans, choopped
3/4 almonds, chopped
4 tablespoons margarine

Cook coconut, pineapple and sugar on low heat in a heavy skillet, stirring constantly until sugar melts. Add nuts to skillet, cooking on low and stirring until evenly distributed, about 5 minutes Add margarine to skillet and mix in. Turn contents into an ovenproof dish and bake at 350 degrees until top is toasted.

Oat-paste a la "Ox"   by Joachim "Ox" Hiller

100 grams oats (medium crushed)
2 tablespoons carob or cocoa
1 pinch of salt
1 pinch of cinnamon
1 teaspoon of vanilla
100 grams water
100 grams honey
100 grams margarine

Mix oats, carob/cocoa, salt, cinnamon, vanilla. Heat water, margarine, and honey until margarine melts. Pour it over the crushed oats and mix it.
[NOTE: 100 grams is equal to a little less than 1/2 cup.]

Jack's Chocolate Pie

2 9" baked pie shells (see piecrust recipes)
2 cups sugar
1/2 cup cornstarch
3 cups soy (not oi) milk (scalded)
1 12 Oz. package Bakers semi-sweet chocolate chips
4 tablespoons vanilla

Combine all the dry ingredients and slowly add scalded milk and mix over HI heat, then switch to medium. As it starts to thicken pour in the bag of chips and try as best as you can to stir the lumps out. Pour into two 9" pie crusts and refrigerate for two hours. Always make two pies at a time because the first one is always gone the night you make it (especially here at the HIPPYCORE hotel). Fair Lanes mate.

← CORDUROY

joel's SIN-amon Rolls
Baking Tunes: anything metal and evil

I bake this for human sacrifices, satanic rituals, pagan dances and other unholy ceremonies, as well as giving a dozen to relatives at Christmas. They taste awesome and they're pretty easy, too.

bread dough (recipe in "Essentials" section)
1 stick margarine
lots of cinnamon
lots of brown sugar

First, follow all the instructions of my bread recipe up to the part where it says "After it has risen a second time. . ." Let it rise twice, but instead of putting the dough in bread pans, cut the dough in half and put one half on your lightly floured counter. If you have a rolling pin, roll the dough out to about 1/4 inch thickness. If you don't, just stretch and flatten it out as best you can (this is what I have to do).

Melt the margarine, then brush it on the flattened out dough. Don't skimp, as this is the "glue" that will make the cinnamon and brown sugar stick to the dough and form a kind of thick "syrup."

Sprinkle gobs of brown sugar and cinnamon over the margarine. Spread it all over the dough so it will be nice and sweet. If you're into gross stuff like raisins or chopped nuts or whatever, I guess this would be the time to add them, but I don't even mess with that junk in my SIN-amon rolls.

Gently roll the dough up like you would a joint or something. Don't let any of the goods inside ooze out.

Cut the roll into 1/2-3/4 inch pieces, then place them on a 1-2 inch deep ungreased pan.

Repeat for the other half of the dough. Let the rolls rise, uncovered, for about an hour and a half in a warm place, then bake for 10-15 minutes at 375 degrees, or until golden brown. If you want, put some powdered sugar frosting on top (mix powdered sugar and water and maybe some other stuff, I don't know). Definitely beyond good and evil.

SNACKS

SUPER SPORADIC SHREDDED WHEAT SNACK

This is one of those snacks that really comes in hand while studying or doing layout. I especially enjoyed it when trying to understand the Kantian notion of analytical judgements but that's another story.

2 cups shredded wheat
1/4 cup margarine
garlic salt to taste
lemon pepper to taste

Melt margarine and pour over shredded wheat. Next sprinkle garlic salt and lemon pepper, Put it in the oven at 350 degrees F about 15 minutes or so. You'll have to trust me on this one I know shredded wheat is absolutely shit otherwise.

Punk Popcorn   **by joel**
    Tunes: Filth 7" or the soundtrack to "Repo Man"

This recipe is a must when you're sitting at home on a mellow (but pissed) Saturday night, sipping homebrew or homeroot beer brew (jack flaked on the recipe for that one) with your pals and watching Suburbia or those Cringer videos.

popcorn
oil (if you're popping corn on the stove or have an oil popper)
margarine
nutritional yeast flakes (available at any decent co-op or grocery)
lemon pepper (a staple at the Hippycore House)

First, pop that fucking corn, a big bowl of it. I personally prefer air popppers cos they use no oil and are real loud, so check your local thrift stores for a good cheap used one. While the corn is popping, melt some margarine (a lot, almost a whole stick). When the corn is popped, ladle about 3/4 of the melted margarine on it. Generously heave on the nutritional yeast and liberally (but not as a Liberal) shake on lemon pepper. Mix it around real good and then dump the remaining margarine and put more yeast and lemon pepper on top; this creates a sort of topping.

I'm Vegan Cos I'm Selfish
by joel

(Slightly revised from an essay I wrote for A Plea for Sanity #1.
Thanks Jess!)

I'm going to ask you to do something completely selfish and
hedonistic. No I'm not kidding, honest. Just for a moment drop your
false liberal altruism and stop venerating those self-sacrificing idols
you cling to so strongly during those heavy debates with your
conservative friends. Fuck Gandhi, fuck MLK, fuck Mother Theresa,
fuck everyone but yourself (and possibly Ayn Rand). Now that
you've stripped yourself of all those religiously induced feelings of
brotherly/sisterly love, look at yourself in the mirror and stare at
the only really important thing in the universe--you. That's right,
baby, you're Number One and proud of it. Your concerns are primary
in this world, so drop the Golden Rule bullshit and admit it. Life is
for your benefit, your fun, your ego.

So, now that you've stripped your human nature down to its
bare nakedness and you've unapologetically seen yourself for what
you really are--a pleasure-seeking egoist--and you realize the world
is here for your benefit, do something about it.

Stop fucking it up.

Stop oppressing your own species.

Stop oppressing other species.

It seems so obvious that I'm surprised I have to chastise you.
Birds don't shit in their nest; why do you? It amazes me that you, in
your best self-centered utilitarian mood, could hurt yourself. Are
you really so myopic that you could believe that taking care of your
wants, your desires, and your ego allows you to engage in practices
that destroy the planet and the species inhabiting it? If you think
taking care of #1 means fucking over your fellow humans to "make it
to the top," fucking over your planet to have a fast car and a houseful
of technological wizardry, and fucking over other species by stuffing
them callously into your mouth, then you're no self-interested egoist.
You are an idiot.

You see, looking out for Number One is great, it's fine, it's what
everybody does. However, the problem lies in defining exactly what
#1 is. Most people, including your carnivourous, earth-raping self, I
assume, define Number One three ways: me, myself, and I. Snap out
of it, Mr./Ms. Me Generationist. Are you so ignorant and befuddled
that you believe you are a lone, autonomous actor completely
independent from the natural world and other human beings? Like
it or not, my dear egoist, we are all dependent on the natural world
for food-shelter-clothing and upon the human world for sex, culture,
and the social interactions that keep us from going crazy. As much
as you hate Mr. Marx and his Commie crap that subjects the
individual to the whims of a mediocre collectivity you have to admit
he was right in his assertion that humans are social beings. Our
humanness derives from our ability to interact with each other and

produce, whether that production involves making food, a toy, an idea, or love.

So perhaps it is becoming clearer that of course everyone is only looking out for Number One, but our definition of Number One is far too narrow. So, my dear individualist, it's becoming apparent that rational self-interest involves not just the caretaking of the individual, but also the individual's domain; that is, his or her living space.

Now that we know the virtue of selfishness involves selfishly looking out for yourself *and* your domain, what now? Well, we have to take our wonderfully rational, self-interested philosophy and engage it in the real world. I could cite hundreds of examples of ways to apply your wonderful new ideology, such as abandoning your materialist lifestyle, denouncing the banality and dehumanization of the mass society you and I live in, smashing capitalism and the destructive Liberal Humanist ideals it perpetuates (ideals that you yourself used to have in your narrow quest for personal profit of the body at the expense of your domain), etc. etc. However, for the sake of keeping things relatively brief, I'll glean one aspect of our new praxis of self-interest and elaborate on it a bit. I'm speaking of the liberation of animals.

There are several reasons why a good egoist like yourself would want to avoid exploiting other creatures. One is the way industrial societies manufacture animal products such as meat, dairy, eggs, leather, pet food, and fur. Simply, such practices destroy your domain. I don't want to waste any more of your precious time burying you in facts, but do you realize that due to livestock production, 65% of the topsoil in the U.S.--your domain--has been eroded? 260,000,000 acres of your forests have been cleared to place meat in the mouths of ignorant humans who actually believe they are "looking out for #1." The number one environmental threat to your American West is livestock grazing, because cows eat almost any plant, cactus or shrub to the dirt, increasing erosion and altering climate patterns, which turn your stunning but fragile deserts into wastelands. Why are you letting callous purveyors of the me-myself-and-I egoism (let's call it false individualism) destroy your space? Your money is being used to subsidize the staggering amounts of water used by the meat and dairy industry. (two industries that are inextricably linked and cannot survive without one another. The rational individualism we all subscribe to entails veganism, not just vegetarianism.) Did you know that the amount of water used to "produce" an average cow could float a destroyer? Did you know that if the government didn't subsidize water used by the meat industry, hamburger would cost $38 a pound? Do you know where all that cow shit goes? I'll tell you: into your rivers, your streams, your drinking water. Why the fuck are you supporting this? Do you think any of this actually benefits you in any way?

Aside from desecrating your domain, the animal industry attacks your body. Heart disease, which will kill half the people reading this, is directly linked to meat and dairy consumption. A recent Cornell study advocated that Americans should eliminate *all* animal products from their diet, because consuming them is wreaking havoc on their health. Women who eat eggs and cheese have a three times greater chance of developing breast cancer than those rational actors that go vegan; these odds also apply to the risk of fatal ovarian cancer. The antibiotics injected into livestock to fatten them up have built up humans' resistance to antibiotics, making them almost useless as medicines. Add to this scenario the fact that animal byproduct consumption has led to the contamination of 99% of all women's milk by the lethal poison DDT (only 8% of veggie women, though) and the reduction of males' sperm count by 30% over the last 30 years and it should be glaringly clear that the animal industry is waging a full-scale war on you. Why do you support it? Why do you pay these industries to kill you? Perhaps even more ludicrously, after they've already poisoned you, why do you support them spending your money and wasting your knowledge and resources in your labs and universities to test on animals in some twisted form of "science" that trys to put a band aid over the head they themselves severed? Do you think this testing, which has yet to cure any of the industrial diseases they've created, benefits you? Come on now, you're not being very rational or self-interested, are you?

That's another thing about this whole animal industry business. It perpetuates the false individualism you used to subscribe to but now know is in fact anti-individualist. We don't see the clearcut forests, the polluted streams, the slash-and-burn tactics applied to the rainforests for grazing pastures, the desertified wastelands, the leghold traps that grab any wildlife unfortunate enough to stand in them, the factory farms that consume immense amounts of grain, water, and petroleum, or the toxic chemicals dumped into our ecosystem by the leather indusry. Instead, we only see a neat cut of tenderloin wrapped in styrofoam and plastic, a shiny pair of Doc Martens, a double cheeseburger dripping with trimmings, a beautiful fox stole. We consume without considering how that consumption affects us, beyond the superficial level of how it hurts our pocketbook or fills our belly. While that Big Mac or cheese pizza may taste deliciously wonderful for those ten minutes of munching, we ignore the deep consequences of our actions and only because we can't see them. If you're really the egoist you claim to be, you'll realize that serving your own interests goes beyond immediate, hedonistic gratification. Sustainment and permanence are the ideals of a real egoist, so that you and your children can be assured of a healthy, life-giving space for generations to come.

Also, by refusing to harm yourself by participating in the hedonistic exploitation of others, you slowly, sinuously and almost unknowingly begin to appreciate the self-interested actions of other beings. You begin to realize that cows, lions, lizards, birds, dolphins, and perhaps even plants are self-interested egoists themselves, looking out for themselves via their interactions within their family unit and/or ecosystem. Once this recognition develops, it is almost beyond comprehension to even imagine exploiting them for your caprices, because one of the absolute principles of your radical individualism is that you can do whatever you want as long as it doesn't infringe upon the rights and interests of others. These creatures are certainly self-interested, and while perhaps not "rational" as defined by humans such as yourself, they nevertheless express a desire to live in their domain unfettered by the idiocy of humans' false individualism, and you can't help but respect that.

As this new notion of individualism attaches itself to the parameters of your mind and begins to develop further, you might slowly begin to notice that the dualism between your body and your domain begins to break down and lose meaning. It becomes increasingly obvious that body and domain are not separate entities, but part of the same whole. The liberation of animals, of the planet from the toxic manacles of industrial capitalism, and of the human species from hierarchies and powers that commodify us into alienated consumers are all related and part of the task of your new individualism. It has become apparent that everything is related. Our domain (and body) is the totality of interacting systems (natural and theoretical), all hopelessly connected to each other in the briar patch of existence. To liberate yourself, you need to liberate everything else, including animals. Hmmm, maybe you're not so selfish after all.

Oven-baked Potato Chips   by Donna Rivest

Baking potatoes, sliced 1/8" thick
Olive oil
pepper

With a pastry brush, brush one side of potato slices with oil.
Place oiled side face down on a baking sheet. Do not overlap slices.
Brush tops of potato with oil. Sprinkle with pepper. Bake 15
minutes at 400 degrees. Turn potatoes over, and bake and additional
10 minutes until crispy. Be careful not to burn. Serve immediately.

Jack's Bodacious Bean Dip

This is a coalating party favorite and is almost always served
as a prerequisite to assembling Hippycore products. In fact, we will
probably be enjoying it while assembling this very book!

1 onion
8 jalepeño peppers
1 32 oz can refried beans (check and make sure it contains no lard)
1 32 oz can chili beans
1 tablespoon cayenne pepper
1 tablespoon chili powder
1 tablespoon crushed red pepper

Dice onions and jalepeño peppers and fry in hot oil in a big pot
until onions are cooked. Add all beans and spices and heat about 15
minutes. Serve with tortilla chips, salsa, etc., and make sure you take
a vegan breath mint after eating this! Whew!

WHY VEGAN? WHY PUNK FOR THAT MATTER...
by j@ck

Well there are a lot of great reasons to be vegan. I remember once telling a girl I was vegan and she said it sounded like something on STAR TREK. "I am vegan, live long and prosper". There was a point at which we started putting together this cook book that I thought it might be important to include scientific, environmental, and factual info on factory farms etc... I even considered using graphic photos to get the point across. Most of you by now already have a fairly good idea about what happens in the factory farms and if you don't we should provide some addresses at the end of this cook book for more info.

And besides Joel is going to tackle the philosophy thing in such great depth that I think anyone that isn't thoroughly convinced to pour their dairy products down the drain must be crazy. So rather than using philosophy, scare tactics, or the like I'm going to tell you a story. Let's call it "The History of J@ck Kahn's eating habits circa 1985 to present" Actually most of this will apply to Joel as well since we made our transitions around the same time.

So it's 1985. I am about 15 years old, in high school, and seriously into heavy metal. (FUCKIN METAL- LeaAnne). I remember in the 8th grade I bought this lobster necklace as a symbol of my allegiance to THE SCORPIONS because I couldn't find any SCORPIONS paraphernalia at the time. About the time I turn 16 years old I have my first serious relationship with a woman (Jennifer) ah yes, puppy love.... In any case this is a time in my life where I was really rethinking my general outlook and lifestyle. I became rather obsessed with Jennifer, not only because she seemed to care about me for me and nothing else.

So I began to blow off all my "metal friends" and behind my back was termed "Pussywhipped". As time went on I realized how little I had in common with them. Not that they were bad people or anything but the whole metal image just didn't seem to fit a somewhat nerdy intellectual like myself.

So by the time my 17th birthday rolled around I bought my first punk rock record. And it is still one of my faves DISCHARGE "Hear Nothing...". Wow! I had met a lot of punks at school and began hanging out with them and they introduced me to all kinds of bands (BGK, CONFLICT, 7 SECONDS, GBH, etc...) and for whatever reason most of the new bands I was listening to had some really great lyrics. No more fantasy death crazed head banging demons for me (well until I met Joel).

I began to feel an identity with the punks and in no time joined a hardcore thrash band called DESECRATION (o.k. - Speed Metal). At that time I was really evolving and growing as a person. I was thinking more in terms of radical politics and it really excited me.

I considered myself a "peace punk" for a while because that seemed to fit me and most of my friends. I wasn't exactly sure what a "peace punk" was but I seemed to hate all the same things that they did so it seemed appropriate enough.

I'm not sure exactly what it took to start considering non human animals in this new philosophy melding in my brain perhaps it was the constant barrage of CONFLICT lyrics, friends that were vegetarian, zines, etc... Eventually I was wholly convinced that something just didn't seem right about eating meat. At this point I had absolutely no facts about it, no good arguments, knew next to nothing about deforestation, thermodynamic laws, factory farming, etc... I just knew as a person that wanted to respect life that (gulp) I'd have to give up meat.

This was nearly impossible for me because at the time I still lived at home and my parents aren't exactly up on new and revolutionary ideas. So I spent several months feeding my flesh portions to our canine pal "Bear" (who loved me even more for it) and throwing the rest of the blood and chunks in the trash. I wasn't embarrassed of my new found feelings but I have a rather odd relationship with my parents (maybe someday I'll write a piece on this) and just didn't think they would understand.

So Joel moved into a shitty apartment with me and we both decided to go full vegetarian. We also became involved with "animal rights". I was fascinated by all the philosophy and intelligent arguments behind the idea of inter species equality and tolerance. We became involved in a local animal rights group and attended demonstrations against the fur industry, meat consumption, cosmetic testing etc... We memorized all the catchy slogans and arguments from the likes of Peter Singer etc... and were quite content. We bought "cruelty free" shampoos, soaps, etc... stuff not tested on animals. Joel was even reluctant to buy those odd leather sex toys but he had to give in to remain consistent.

So Joel and I started out as what would later be known as "Junk food vegetarians". By this I mean we basically eliminated meat from our diets without replacing it. Our diets consisted of a lot of Heinz Veggie beans, mac n' cheese, pizza, burritos etc.. It was fun for a while...

I'll never forget this conversation we had with a local band that we were interviewing fir HIPPYCORE. For whatever reason animal rights issues came up and one of the band members asked what were our reasons for not being vegan (v.s. just vegetarian although I don't believe any of them are vegan at this time). We really didn't have a good answer. All of our arguments for being vegetarian seemed to include veganism as the next step. "Well I suppose we are lazy" or "We can't live without dairy it just can't be done" were typical responses.

The "lazy" excuse worked for about two months but anyone that knows Joel or I could hardly describe either of us as lazy (metal maybe but lazy no way). We could justify it no more. One summer (about 2 1/2 years ago) we decided when we returned from our trip to the Bay area our home would be dairyless. No more DAIRY QUEEN, no more PIZZA, no more CHEEZ... life seemed pretty dismal but the struggle continued.

It was difficult at first and we didn't have a handy dandy cookbook like the one you're holding either. The interesting thing about being vegan is that it compels you to be creative. No more slop together 1-2-3- cheese sandwiches. Being vegan forces you to think which I know scares some people. Most people don't want to think about what they eat, they just want to eat. I know that eating is just another bodily function but it seems to me we should think about everything we do (sex is a good example to prevent diseases eh?) anything worth doing requires a little thought so what the hell? For us creating and experimenting in the kitchen is a blast not a chore what so ever.

So now we have vegan party pot lucks and cook all kinds of crazy food for all kinds of crazy people. We've even cooked vegan delights for some very vicious carnivores (you know who you are) that had to admit the food was quite palatable. Even hardcore carnivores have complimented us on our culinary expertise.

So why be vegan? It's never been our philosophy to tell anyone what to do. What we've hoped to do is provide an alternative to MC DONALDS flesh burgers and KENTUCKY FRIED hacked off body parts. Being vegan for me is a fun and creative way to live my life and I do

it not only because it seems right on philosophically but also because I enjoy doing it. So why not?

Love and animal liberation, j@ck

The Ultimate Salsa   **by Tom Messmer**

1 tomato
1/2 cup chopped onion
1 scallion
1 tablespoon red jalepeno relish (or other jalepeno stuff)
2 tablespoons vinegar (red wine is best)

Chop everything up into fairly small chunks, and mix it all up.
Eat with corn chips, burritos, during sex, etc.

TOFU VEGGIE DIP

I remember once asking Chris Of Equals to make this at an HC
party but he was too much of a HE MAN for cooking and passed it
onto Erica. She did a wonderful job although she didn't like it, I did
so there.

1 block tofu
1 clove garlic minced
1 teaspoon vinegar
3 teaspoons soy (Need I say more, not oi) sauce
3 tablespoons lemon juice
4 tablespooons garlic salt
4 tablespoons black pepper
1/4 cup water
1/4 cup olive oil

Put all this in a blender and mix. Cool at least two hours before
serving with your favorite veggies. Hubba Hubba!

Roasted Red Peppers in Olive Oil   by Jackie Weltman

Preheat oven to 500 degrees. Place ripe red sweet peppers on a lightly greased baking sheet in the oven. Roast until skins blacken and blister, then turn to ensure even roast. The entire pepper doesn't have to turn black, but a large part of the skin should blister. When this is done, remover peppers and place in a closed brown paper bag ten minutes to steam. Then remove and deseed and remove skin by hand. Discard skin. Do not rinse peppers. It's sticky; just wash your hands later. When seeded and peeled, slice peppers into strips and cover with the best extra virgin olive oil you can find. Add (preferably fresh) marjoram and rosemary leaves. Marinate several hours and inhale 'em as is!

Taratour Sauce

1/4 cup tahini
1 small clove garlic, pressed or minced
1/8 cup fresh lemon juice
1/4   teaspoon salt
1/8 cup cold water

Mix tahini and garlic first, then add remaining ingredients.

"Herb" Tea   by Max

Don't throw away all those seeds and stems when you clean your herb.

Tie up all the waste from your stash into a muslim ball or a piece of cheesecloth. (Quantity will determine potency.)

Drop cheesecloth into kettle of water, and bring water to a boil. Allow kettle to boil for a few minutes, then remove from flame and let it steep for another five minutes with herb still inside.

Add sugar and lemon to taste, and drink up!